Transitions

What people are saying:

"Jean Long Manteufel has a way of reaching deep into your soul with her meaningful, relevant and timeless articles.

I especially enjoyed the letter opener article because it brought back wonderful memories of my childhood and watching my mother opening the mail each day with a special letter opener. Today I have that letter opener and think of my mother every time I use it. Thank you, Jean, for the memories."

**- Kathy Keene, Radio Talk Show Host,
WHBY's Good Neighbor Show**

"A favorite read in our family - Jean's columns are always practical, to the point and written from her wealth of knowledge and life experiences. Jan and I will enjoy sharing this collection with our friends and family."

- John and Jan Gillespie, Founders, Rawhide Boys Ranch

"Jean Long Manteufel has written a remarkable collection of essays about her work with older adults in transition. Jean's keen insight and engaging writing style makes this book a must-read for professionals working with older adults, seniors themselves, and their family members. Jean's book is positive, practical and chock-full of useful information!"

**- Mary Kay Buysse, Executive Director,
National Association of Senior Move Managers®**

"These stories show a real vision into the world of children facing real life challenges with aging parents. On a personal level, many of the stories hit the mark for what my brothers, sisters, and I have been experiencing with our parents."

- Patrick Leigl, Social Services Director, The Salvation Army – Fox Cities

"Jean Long Manteufel is an ambassador of knowledge for the sandwich generation. Her 'how to' stories about aging parents are truly enlightening, enriching and action provoking. A must-read if you're looking for ways to navigate the rocky road of aging parents. Jean's book speaks to having a mature, respectful and FUN relationship with your parents as they age."

- Amy Jo Powers, Regional Manager of Business Development, Heartland Home Health

"When Mom or Dad has dementia, they don't need you less. They need you different. Jean's insights will inspire you to change the way you think and behave, helping you relax and enjoy moments with your loved one."

- Jason J. Schmitz, RN., Owner/Founder, Heartwood Senior Living, Appleton, WI

"Jean connects with her readers just as she does with everyone she meets. She is always professional, courteous and honest. What distinguishes her from any other "professional" is that she does her work in a caring and loving way. She brings heart to her work, this is not a job, but a calling to help others transition."

- Mito Kudaka, Peace Corps Volunteer, Albania 2013

Transitions

*Stories of how to help Mom and Dad
with their stuff*

Jean Long Manteufel

Illustrations by Gladie Long

Cover photo by Mike Manteufel

Cover design by Sam Needham

Copyright © 2014   Jean Long Manteufel

First edition, first printing

ISBN-13: 978-0692253274 (Grandma Fav Publishing)
ISBN-10: 0692253270

Library of Congress Control Number: 2014913261
Grandma Fav Publishing,   Appleton WI

(920)734-3260
TransitionsWithJean.com

DEDICATION

To my hubby, Randy - my love and my life. Yeah!

To my wonderful parents, Jerry and Gladie Long, who taught us to live joyfully. Mom and Dad, you have always been awesome role-models.

"If you didn't laugh, you'd cry –
and laughing is just more fun!"

- *Mom*

ACKNOWLEDGEMENTS

My special thanks to Dan Flannery and Ed Berthiaume
from the Post Crescent for giving me the opportunity to
write a monthly column about the challenges faced by
seniors and their boomer children.

Thanks to my friends, Chuck Wagner and Keith Zentner, as well
as my sister, Laura Muinde, who always took the time to check
over my columns before they were published. Their input
was appreciated and sometimes quite amusing.

My gratitude to Adrienne Simpson and Amy Jo Powers
for getting me started as a Senior Move Manager.
It was a wonderful gift.

Thanks to author Renee Beese for taking a newbie under wing.

Mom, thanks for doing the illustrations. I'm honored.

Everyone should have their own cheering section – people who
give you their enthusiastic support. Seated in the front row of
mine are Ann Sensenbrenner Salutz, Earl Zwicker, Bob Brandt
and Tom Rigden.

Finally, thanks to my Mom and Dad, who good-naturedly smile
when their friends ask if I'm writing about them. Of course not.
These tales are about shared challenges that most families face
at one time or another.

i

INTRODUCTION

In 1917, my grandpa, Harry H. Long, brought milk in from the family farm and delivered it to town with his horses and wagon.

Grandpa would then go to the Soo Line and pick up orders from Sears & Roebuck or Montgomery Wards and deliver goods to folks in Appleton. That was how Grandpa and Grandma (Alice Long) started Harry H. Long Moving & Storage.

Dad grew up working there, and in 1960, my parents, Jerry and Gladie Long, started their own delivery service, A-1 Cartage. Because they ran the business from our house, we eight children learned early on about packing, moving and helping care for our customers.

I am a third-generation mover. Today, my son, Mike, and I own A-1 Moving & Storage.

Seniors have always been my favorite customers. If they call to move, and are having an especially difficult time, I want to make their transition easier. Some of them really need help.

Leaving the house they've been in for 50-plus years, often because of declining health or death of a spouse, means making change at a time when they are not their strongest.

Often they are overcome by the workload. They don't know where to start. Many times they break down in tears.

In 2007, I learned about a group that gives exactly this kind of assistance, the National Association of Senior Move Managers. I attended their training and became a Certified Relocation and Transition Specialist (CRST).

We started a new business - Long's Senior Transitions.

Senior Move Management is not only about the moving. We are experts at helping with the emotion and commotion as we guide folks through the transition from the big family house to their new home, wherever that home may be.

We help them deal with all the stuff - whether it is the physical stuff in their home or the emotional stuff that they must face.

In May, 2010, the Appleton Post Crescent gave me the opportunity to write a monthly column to help guide seniors and their boomer children through these transitions.

This is a collection of columns, with updates and additions. Customers' names and identifying characteristics are changed.

The stories aren't just one person's story. If it feels familiar, it is because there are many of us sharing the same experiences.

Hopefully, when you read these pages, you will get ideas for yourself or to share with your family and friends.

Now get that highlighter out. Let's get going!

1 THINGS TO CONSIDER DURING LIFE'S EMOTIONAL TRANSITIONS

Sinatra said it best when he sang: "I Did It My Way."

Seniors, right now, do you feel that you are living your life your way?

As you are getting older, are you finding the house you raised your family in is becoming too much to take care of, but you don't want to leave your home?   Are you independent and determined to stay that way?   Have you considered moving out of your house, but are absolutely overwhelmed with the work it will take to clear out 50 years of stuff, so you just don't deal with it? Possibly your health has started to worry you, or your spouse's health.   Perhaps you find yourself needing more help dealing with things that used to be pretty easy.

Or, maybe you have already set yourself up so that you're able to spend time enjoying whatever it is you like and are able to do.   When your children and grandchildren come over, you visit and share what is going on in your life.   You get to enjoy their stories about what is going on with them.

You are busy doing things that are fun. You are living the good life that you dreamed you would have when you retired.

Those of you readers who are adult children of seniors, are you getting much more involved in helping Mom and Dad? Are you worried about their safety? Do you try to tell them what to do, but they just won't listen? Maybe taking care of your mom and dad is straining the relationship between you and your brothers and sisters. Consider how it is affecting your spouse. Are you becoming exhausted? Do you need help but don't know where to turn?

Now, you have help.

Mom and Dad, you worked hard all your life so that you could enjoy your retirement. We want to explore ways to make that happen. It is all about choices, your choices, your way.

Let me be your coach. In each column, I'll address some specific challenges that folks like you (and I) are facing, and I'll guide you with suggestions you might want to try. Huddle up with your team of family and friends. Talk it over. Discuss what works for you and create a plan for yourself. As we go along, you'll get ideas on how you can tackle some of the obstacles that come your way. Ask questions. We'll keep encouraging you. You might want to move at a fast pace or take it slow, but you will be the one in control.

We'll go through this together. You aren't alone. Best of all, I promise, you'll be a winner because you will be doing it your way.

2   LISTEN WHEN PARENTS WANT TO TALK ABOUT DOWNSIZING

"I am so mad at my mom!" I was recently told by a friend.

"Why?" I asked.

"Because she sold Grandma's rocker,"   she replied angrily. "Mom asked me three times if I wanted it. Of course I said no, because I knew how much it meant to Mom. Then Mom turned around and sold it!"

Wow, talk about miscommunication. There was so much underlying emotion going on in that conversation that they just weren't hearing each other.

More or less, Mom was saying: "I won't be around forever. It is time to start clearing out the house. Grandma's rocker is very special to me. I want it to stay in the family, and I want you to have it."

All that the daughter heard Mom saying was: "I won't be around forever." The daughter didn't want to think about a future without Mom, so she stopped listening.

Parents, you brought your children up to be kind, giving and loving. When you ask: "Do you want my china?" they will usually say no. Not because they don't want it one day in the future, they probably do, but they don't want to take it away from you if they know you love it.

Often parents will ask if the kids want something. Children are very uncomfortable with this conversation because it means considering a future where Mom and Dad aren't there anymore.

Parents, here are some ideas on how to be in control of what happens to your possessions.

Hints are not sufficient. Make it crystal clear. Have a sit-down with your children or send a letter. Say something like: "Kids, we are looking toward our future. We are starting to downsize the house, and we need your help. "

Set a deadline. Not too long, not too short, maybe a month or two. Tell them: "The deadline is X. After that, we will be getting rid of anything that we don't want that isn't spoken for. If there is something you want, speak now, or forever hold your peace ."

Parents, share a list of the items you want to keep for now, and that aren't available.

Kids, when Mom and Dad ask if you want anything, it's because they have many possessions that they love and have enjoyed over the years. They want those items to go to someone who will also love them, and share their history.

Don't dismiss your parents. Don't put them off by insisting that you don't need to have this conversation for many years. Help them.

Work together with Mom and Dad. Work together with your siblings. Be respectful of your parents' possessions and their feelings.

Enjoy this time of sharing. Don't steamroll. Give your parents time to say goodbye to things they love. Listen to Mom's and Dad's stories.

Being able to do this together is a special gift - one you will remember for many years to come. Be helpful and be kind.

3   SIMPLE STEPS TO MAKE PARENTS' HOME A LITTLE BIT SAFER

"I want to stay in my house!" Jeepers. I hear that almost every week from seniors I work with.

You may hear that same thing from your parents.

Today we won't debate whether your parents should stay in their home, rather, considering that 40% of admissions to nursing homes are due to falls, let's simply look at ways to lessen the risk of them falling.

Let's help them live in their house safer. Maybe look to your own house with some of these ideas in mind.

My pal, Nancy Krueger, at the Aging and Disability Resource Center, says the biggest reason people fall at home is because of hurrying or not paying attention; for example, trying to get to the phone in time or doing two things at once. Talk together about slowing down and paying more attention.

Medicine also plays a huge role in falling. We will discuss that at another time.

Let's take a look around their house together. First, every place where there are steps there should be a stable handrail, including at the garage and outside the front door.

Folks, do you clutter up the stairs with things that are "going to go up"? Clear the steps off once and for all. Put a chair near the stairs, but out of the way, and stack the items there for those trips. Don't let pets sleep on the stairs. Install a phone in the basement near the stairs, reachable from the floor.

Thirty percent of falls happen in the living room. It's where we spend most of our time, and where we are the most relaxed, which means we are paying less attention. Make sure the chair that they use has good arms that give sturdy support when getting up. Get rid of all clutter and excess furniture. Make sure there are good, open walkways.

In the kitchen, stay off those dang stools. Empty those cupboards that are beyond reach. Put things that are often used on the counter for easy access.

Next, let's check the bedroom. Again, are the paths clear? We all get up at night to use the bathroom. Make sure there is a sturdy night stand and good lighting so they can see where they are stepping.

In the bathroom, have someone who is handy install grab-bars everywhere they need them. A towel bar is not a grab-bar. Have a phone reachable for emergencies. Eliminate slippery surfaces. Get rid of those darn scatter rugs. Talk about a tripping hazard! I can hear people saying: "But I like them." Remind them why we are doing this. Our goal is making the home safe so they can stay there longer.

If your parents tell you they want to stay in their house, discuss it with them, and if you both agree it can be done, work together to make their house safer from falling hazards.

Contact your local Aging and Disability Resource Network.

For information about your local Aging and Disability Resource Network, see: www.adrc-tae.acl.gov

If you are in Wisconsin: http://www.dhs.wisconsin.gov/adrc/

4 THERE COMES A TIME WHEN OUR 'STUFF' IS TOO MUCH

Every time I use the "S" word in this column, my mom just cringes. "Why do you keep saying 'stuff' in your stories?" She asks me. To her, referring to people's personal possessions as "stuff" is disrespectful.

On one hand, Mom is right. As a third-generation professional mover and a Certified Moving Consultant®, I never say "stuff" to describe household goods. It is rude. We refer to a customer's possessions as their "items". Never, ever as their "stuff".

On the other hand, now I have this second business helping seniors and boomers to downsize their homes. In their own words, and every single day, they tell us they have so much stuff that they don't know where to start.

As a noun, "stuff" refers to objects in general. It also refers to worthless objects - refuse; junk. After 70 years of collecting, one can have many objects in general, and by their sheer volume, they become worthless to a person who no longer uses them.

As a verb, stuff means to fill too full - overload; cram. A second way it is used as a verb means to plug-up or block something.

When I use the word stuff I mean a little bit of each of those descriptions, but never to speak of peoples' cherished items.

First, there is the stuff that is just random things people own that they neither care about, nor love and enjoy. It just exists in their space. They have "stuff in the basement" that they need to get rid of.

Second, there is the full-to-overflowing use. "This house is stuffed with things we don't use anymore."

The third way I use it is the one that is the real troublemaker, when their stuff becomes an obstacle.

Do you have this third kind of stuff in your life? Have you considered moving somewhere else, but can't because you have to deal with the stuff?

Is your house so full of stuff that you spend too much time cleaning, clearing or just feeling overwhelmed?

It's not just inside, but outside, too. A yard can be an obstacle when it becomes a burden to care for it. Maybe you are no longer able to readily maintain your house, but stay there because it holds all your stuff.

When your kids stop over, do you play cards or go out to eat, enjoying each other's company or do they spend their time fixing, washing and cutting your stuff?

At some point, our items go from being the fruits of a lifetime of collecting to becoming a hindrance to living comfortably.

Then, worse, how many families have you seen torn apart because when the parents are gone, the children fight over who gets which stuff?

The material things of our life are taking over what is really important.

Are we giving our stuff too much control over us?

So, Mom, in the *Transitions* column, yes, we absolutely spend most of our time helping folks deal with their stuff! It's what we do.

5 VIDEO: A GREAT WAY TO PRESERVE A LIFETIME OF MEMORIES

One of the ways we preserve our memories is by keeping items that remind us of something or someone special.

Look around you. How many objects, right there, remind you of a person or an event? Now multiply that by five or six decades, and you begin to see why Mom won't part with anything.

Several years ago, I received a call from Harold. He thought he needed my help, but said he was "not ready to say good-bye".

He explained. Five years before, he had lost Mary, his wife of 60 years. He had already sold the house and moved to assisted living. He still had whole rooms that held memories for him, so he had rented another apartment just to store their special possessions.

His three sons lived out of state. They didn't want anything. "Get rid of that junk, Dad," they said. Ouch.

He took me through his place, proudly pointing out items and reminiscing. "This is the vase we bought on our honeymoon," and "Mary's parents gave us this china for our wedding." Even, "My dad and I made this table when I was in 8th grade."

He took me through 60 years of memories. He was near tears several times. No wonder he couldn't part with anything.

Thinking about him that night, I had an idea. The next day, I got out my yellow pages, and found Charles Boesen, a videographer at Lifetime Image. I explained what I wanted. "Walk through the apartment with Harold while making a video," I said. "Ask him about things as you go. Have him share his memories. In the bedroom closet, there are just two dresses. Ask their significance. Don't spend lots of money editing. Just keep it simple."

Then I talked to Harold and suggested that he create a video memory. He did.

Afterward, he was a little more able to clear out the contents, because he could still relive the memories by watching the DVD.

There was an unforeseen benefit. He had sent copies to his sons, and they called! "Dad, can I have Mom's china?" one asked. "May I have the table you and Grandpa made?" another asked. They requested quite a few items, which Harold was pleased to pass on.

What I'm suggesting is that you help your parents make a video memory.

Don't just show up. Ask them ahead of time. Plan on it taking an hour. Have them point out items that have meaning to them and tell why. Special items are usually in the living room, dining room, kitchen and their bedroom. Let them talk.

You can also do it in an interview style. Have someone shoot the video, and you can do the interviewing. By doing it that way, you can guide them along a little.

Use a tripod to keep steady, or ask one of the grandkids to help. They're probably better at electronics anyway, and it'll be a memory they'll cherish.

If your parents don't want to do it, ask if you may do it yourself. You grew up in that house, so you also have memories there worth preserving. Your folks might surprise you by jumping in once you get going.

You'll have a beautiful new memory that you all created together. Do it. Soon.

6 WHEN LIFE'S MOMENTS HAPPEN, BE THERE

"Don't just do something, stand there!"

That was the theme of a presentation given by the Rev. Peter Brinkman at an inspiration celebration I attended almost a decade ago.

He talked eloquently, and, yes, inspirationally, about the importance of just showing up for people, of simply "being there."

A light went on. I had always known it deep down, but never heard it put into words.

Listening to Brinkman brought back many memories.

My Grandma Long had 40 grandchildren. She attended every baptism, wedding and funeral. I remembered seeing her at my First Communion. She was always there.

When Randy and I were married, I remembered that, as we stood at the altar to say our vows, I looked out at the people who showed up for the Mass and thought, "Wow, this is wonderful. Look who is here. There is even my cousin, Jeff, and my friend, Marcia." No, I didn't remember everyone who was there, but I remembered the love.

From then on, I promised myself to make the wedding ceremonies when invited, not just the receptions.

When I graduated from UWGB as a returning adult, after four years of studying, working and trying to be a good wife and mother, my family was there. My brother, Tom, even came from California just to share the moment with me. They were all there, and I remembered.

Later, when I was recovering from surgery, there were six long weeks stuck at home. Ugh. My buddy, Pat, showed up and walked around the block with me. Thanks, Pat. That's a real friend. I still remember it.

Now I've reached the point in my life when friends are no longer in the hospital having babies, but rather are in the hospital recovering from surgeries and having health issues. There are more funerals than weddings.

The Lord has truly blessed my family because we still have our parents here with us. Yes, we do know how fortunate we are.

This week, I was reminded of the importance of being there.

At the office, I mentioned that there is a funeral on Sunday for a friend, and that I didn't think I should go because I don't know any of his family. I wouldn't know what to say to them.

"Go!" Said one of my co-workers, who had the sad experience of losing her mom. She corrected me adamantly. "Go. You don't know how much it means to the family," she explained. "We don't remember everyone who was there, but we remember the caring and the love. It meant so much to us to hear from people who knew Mom."

Rev. Brinkman passed away this January. Fittingly, on the cover of his memorial booklet, his words were shared again: "Don't just do something, stand there!"

He inspired me then, as he still inspires me today. I'll be going to that friend's funeral. Afterward, I think I'll go visit my buddy, Jim, who is in a nursing home.

Thanks, Rev. Brinkman, for reminding me of the importance of being there.

After this column came out, reader Nancy added: "It really is the kind acts of love that you don't think are important that mean the world to the person who is grieving. When my cousin Julie brought over subs after my sister died – she thought it was so minor, but it really meant so much to me."

Another reader reminds us: "Being there doesn't necessarily mean being there in person. If you don't live nearby, hearing from someone in any way is greatly appreciated."

7 ENGAGING IN LIFE AT ANY AGE WILL BRING ADDED ENJOYMENT

"Think about the amount of living you did between the ages of 25 and 55. I would guess you did an immense amount of living during those years. Why do we view ages 65 to 95 differently?"

That was part of a commercial I heard on the radio. It was Amy Jo Powers, from Touchmark Retirement Community in Appleton. It really struck me.

In the commercial, she also said seniors should: "Keep dreaming, keep doing and stay active."

Shortly after that, I heard 76-year-old Florence Henderson, a.k.a. Mrs. Brady, on "Dancing With the Stars". She said that seniors should "stay interested and stay interesting."

Amen!

One of the very toughest questions I often hear is: "When should Mom/Dad move out of the house and into a senior community?"

The first and obvious answer is when they can no longer safely stay at home.

Today, let's look at a second reason: When they become socially isolated.

When you are cut off from the social world, your world itself becomes a smaller place.

Moms and dads, do you have only one "event" going on this week? Maybe it's a doctor's appointment, but is it all that is happening?

When your life becomes uneventful, you become less interested. You retreat physically and mentally. Sitting in front of the television from the time you wake in the morning until you go to bed at night does not keep you interested. You feel lonely because you are.

Have you told your family that you want to stay in your house? That you want to stay independent? Think about it. Are you really independent or just alone? Do you live for the day the children and grandchildren come and then spend their visit reprimanding them for not coming more often? Are you interesting to them when they are there, telling them about activities you have going on?

You still have a lot of life to live. If you're lonely, consider moving to a community. Every single person that we have moved has said that the transition itself was difficult, but now that they are at their new home, their life is full of new activities, they feel more independent than they have been in years, and they have new friends. Their only regret is not doing it sooner.

Your day could start by having breakfast with friends. Maybe there is a morning activity like yoga or choir. Guys, you can go work in the shop and putter around, have lunch with one of your buddies and a card game in the afternoon, knowing that when you want privacy, you can enjoy the solitude in your own apartment.

Yes, it is a lot of emotional and physical work getting there, but throughout life, haven't you found that anything worth having is worth working for?

Besides, these are the seniors who, when their kids come to visit, just might not be home. They are busy doing things.

Like Mrs. Brady asked: Are you interested and interesting?

8   WILL IT BE A FAMILY MEMORY OR A TRAIN WRECK?

Nancy told me that her mom has big plans this month – the whole family is going camping for a week.

Mom thinks it will be wonderful for Nancy and her brother, Joe, along with their spouses and kids, to sit around the campfire, roast marshmallows and sing songs. She thinks it will be a great way to bond and pull the family together.

Nancy is 43 years old, and has two teenagers. The kids want to know if they can just stay home. Her husband is willing to go along if he has to, but only for a long weekend. He isn't taking off work to go camping.   Nancy, who is already dreading the trip, wants to make it work because it means so much to Mom.

Joe's idea of roughing it is to bake his own pizza instead of having it delivered. He is 45 and has never been camping. His wife is also willing to go along if she has to, but asked if they can just stay at a nearby hotel, then go visit at the campground.

I had to chuckle as Nancy was telling me this. We can all see how this might turn out.

Nancy just shook her head and laughed too. It's like she knew she was heading into a train wreck, but didn't know how to avoid the inevitable crash.

For Mom to put together all of these elements, then expect a glorious outcome, means she watched too many episodes of "The Donna Reed Show."

This scenario reminds me of a family I had met with. Their dad had just passed away. His children were preparing for the funeral that was coming up in a few days. Because most of them had come from out of town, they were decided to spend that in-between time clearing out the house.

They were sorting, selecting and arguing. The tension in the house was palpable. Some were just going along with whatever was happening because they didn't want to make waves. One was trampling over everyone's emotions. Some had their own children there, helping themselves to items. And, through it all, they kept calling one brother who was making the drive up from Georgia, to include him in on the decisions of who gets what.

It wasn't going well.

Often, without any preparation, families have the trauma of losing a parent, then there's the funeral, and in the midst of all that emotion, they need to be civil, mature and arrive at a fair and equitable distribution of the estate – without hurting anyone's feelings. Ha.

Are you one of those parents who thinks you don't need to make any plans for when your estate is divided between your children? I can't count how many times I've heard: "My children can take care of that when I'm gone."

Do you think that your kids are perfect little angels, who always get along, and that they will join hands, and sing Kumbaya?

Look at all of the families you know that were torn apart by handling their parents' estate, sometimes taking years to overcome the hard feelings that resulted.

So, back to the camping trip, are Mom's expectations realistic? If her goal is to create a memory with her entire family, could she put plans in place that would actually make it a special event for them all to remember?

And, as for Mom's children, spouses, and grandchildren; they have it in their power to create something that the whole family will fondly remember. They also have the power to make it a nightmare.

I wonder how the trip will go.

9   KEEPING PARENTS UPRIGHT MAY TAKE A LITTLE FORESIGHT

Recently I met with a group of folks to help plan a fall prevention event. It's called: *"Don't Let the Fear of Falling Get You Down".*

With a title like that, you know they're a creative bunch!

The idea started because Governor Jim Doyle declared September to be Fall Prevention Awareness Month.   These healthcare professionals want to help keep you and your parents safe.

Did you know that one in four adults over 65 fall each year? A couple columns ago, I shared thoughts on how to make your parents' home environment a safer place. Well, there is a second part to preventing falls. In addition to changes to their house, they can also make personal changes to be safer. Today we'll talk about some of those.

Medication management is the most serious challenge that I've heard in all discussions about falling.   Anyone on four or more medications (most seniors) has a greater risk of falling. Here are a few suggestions.   First, use one pharmacy for all prescriptions - they can catch adverse drug interactions. Second, have a list of all medications your parents take and why they take them.   Bring that list to all doctor appointments (my buddy just puts them all in a bag and totes them along). Finally, know the side effects of all those medications.

Be aware that alcohol affects balance and control. Even one drink, mixed with certain medications, can greatly reduce balance.

Keep up on vision checks. Wearing smudged glasses can cause visual impairment. The new, fashionable eyeglasses that many people are wearing have wide, decorative sides. They act like blinders, taking away your peripheral vision. Get rid of them, Mom! I love you, and your safety is more important than style.

Check with your local first responders and find out if they use File of Life, then put one on the fridge. In a crisis, it tells rescue workers all important information including the emergency contact, doctor, preferred hospital and allergies to medications.

Get an in-home emergency monitoring system – you just push a button and an alert goes out to a family member and/or 911. A real must-have for people who live alone.

Encourage your parents to exercise more to improve balance and strength. We need to stay active to climb stairs.

Buy a calendar, with large print and help keep appointments in order. When you call to tell Mom/Dad about an appointment, ask them to get the calendar while you wait. Be patient while they write it down.

Remind them that when they get up at night, they should get into the habit of first sitting up, then counting to 10, before standing. It stabilizes the blood pressure.

Consider a tai chi or yoga class. Both help with balance, strength and flexibility.

Parents, if you should be using a walker, but won't because of vanity, please reconsider. Think about your long-term goal. If you want to maintain your independence longer, you have to take care of yourself. If you fall and break a bone, you may not have the same choices that you do now.

This may seem like a lot to consider, but isn't it just common sense steps to ensure that all of your steps are safe?

10 KIDS NEED TO TAKE STUFF FROM PARENTS' BASEMENT

You can help your parents with step number 1 of clearing out their house.

Recently I was helping a customer move from one senior community in town to another. After she showed me what she was moving, she remembered that there was more in a basement locker. I was surprised because she seemed well-organized and had extra room in the closets of her current apartment.

"What's in the basement?" I asked.

"My son's stuff," she replied.

"Whoa," I responded. "If you're 92, how old is your son?"

"He's 64," she said. "I keep asking him, but he never comes and gets his stuff."

I told her to call him and let him know he has two weeks to come and get it. No more excuses.

Kids, it is time to go to your parents' house and get your stuff.

I've also had kids tell me that they've told their mom to throw out their items. Why should she? If it is your stuff, it is your job, not hers. News flash: Mom isn't going to throw out your high-school yearbook or your teddy bear. Help her. Go over with bags and boxes and get your stuff.

Kids say they don't have anything at Mom's. Really? Nothing?

Often, when I am scheduled to speak in front of a group, adult children bring their parents to get them thinking about clearing out the house. I tell the audience: "Kids, raise your hand if you have stuff at your parents' house." Never is a hand raised. Then I ask: "Parents, who has stuff at their house that belongs to their kids?" Almost every parent's hand goes up.

Why do you think that is? It's because we just won't give Mom and Dad permission to clear out the things we want. It may be something sentimental (your old desk) or something you think is perfectly useful (the spinet they got for your piano lessons). If you find yourself saying the words: "Mom, you can't get rid of that," you're not helping. You are creating an obstacle for her. If she wants to get rid of something and it has meaning to you, ask for it.

Then go get it. Now.

Yes, there are times when you can reasonably expect Mom and Dad to store items for you such as when you're in college or in your first apartment. But once you have bought your own house, you need to clear out theirs.

An unacceptable excuse is that you moved away. If you own a house in Texas or Timbuktu and still have stuff at Mom's, go home and deal with it. Why should she be burdened with your things? Help her out.

I know your old bedroom is special to you. It is like a shrine to your youth. But maybe if you help her clear it out, she can start feeling the burden lifted from the weight of all the work in the house.

Moms and dads, tear this column out. Write on it: "Come get your stuff." Send it to your kids. They'll get the message.

11   IT'S TIME TO STEP UP AND HELP WITH HOLIDAY GATHERINGS

Let's talk turkey. Today, I'm proposing a very radical idea. Before you shut me down, hear me out.

Thanksgiving and Christmas are right around the corner. Who's making the dinner?

Do you still all converge on your 70- to 80-year-old mom for the holidays to enjoy her wonderful meals? I'll let you in on a little secret: It's a lot of work.

If your mom is 70, then possibly you are 30 to 50. It's time to shape up. Help.

Moms out there, you show your love by making food. For my generation, it is about sharing (which you taught us). We want to share and enjoy the holiday with you. Let us help in a significant way. Let go a little.

The real work is in the dishes that are homemade. Give a grandchild the recipe for your cranberry relish and have him/her make it. They may not get it perfect the first year, but it will become their specialty and a family tradition can really be carried on.

Guys, has your mom asked you to help, but you answer that the game is on? You can help out before and after the game. Yes, you can.

Men, teach your own children how to appreciate the women in your life. After dinner, push the cooks out of the kitchen and clean up. "That's a lot of work," you say. No kidding.

Years ago, my mom told us it was all just too much. She handed over her roasting pans. Now my sister and I make the turkeys. Everyone over 18 years old brings something. Mom and Dad supply the house and the wine. We bring everything else, even the milk. There are 45 of us for dinner. We don't let Mom raise a finger. And it is still a lot of work for her.

If your family has six people, it is even more work for Mom.

Each year it just gets harder, and it's expensive. Bringing a bottle of wine, or the dinner rolls, really isn't enough.

Many of you might be saying: "But Mom *loves* to cook! She would be offended if we suggested anything like you're proposing Jean."

You might be right. Have you asked her?

My wonderful mother-in-law has pampered us for over 30 years. She always puts on a superb Christmas feast.

Last November, I told my hubby that it was time to start very gently suggesting to his mom that, not then, but maybe the next year, she should consider letting us host Christmas dinner. We wanted to approach this delicate subject very carefully because we didn't want to hurt her feelings. We just wanted to start her thinking about it.

After hubby hemmed and hawed around it, and finally got to the point, her eyes lit up, and to our amazement she replied: "Do we have to wait until next year? How about this Christmas?!"

Ask your mom if you can help. You may surprise her. She may surprise you.

12   LISTEN AND OBSERVE WHEN VISITING YOUR PARENTS

Are you heading home for Christmas? Has it been awhile since you've seen Mom or Dad?

Maybe they keep telling you everything is fine with them, but you've started wondering if it really is. Possibly your in-town sibling has said there are problems. Do not dismiss their concerns.

I thought this would be a good time to ask an expert what to look for. As people have been doing for over 100 years, I called the Valley VNA. I met with Pam Hillmann, RN, who is a client care coordinator.

"The key is to be observant, without being invasive," Hillmann explained. "It doesn't take a detective to know things just aren't right. What you are looking for is *change*. Observe if there are any *changes* that can jeopardize your parents' safety."

Pam suggested we take an imaginary visit together.

When your parents greet you, notice how they look, how they sound and act. Are they clean and dressed appropriately? This is where the key word *"change"* comes in. What we really mean is, "are they clean and dressed appropriately *for them."* If Dad has always worn that ratty old sweater, it isn't a *change.*

When you enter the house, look around. Is it normal? Are there piles of bills that haven't been dealt with? Is it their regular level of cleanliness?

Listen as you chat with them.

Are they still talking about current friends, and about their usual activities like church, or bridge, or whatever they normally have done?

Are they in the here and now?

Discuss how things are going with their health.

Play a game of cards or a game you both enjoy. It is a great way to check out their cognitive skills – plus, it's just plain fun! Remember, you're only checking things out. This isn't an inquisition.

Look at their pills. If they are all outdated, they may not be taking their prescriptions.

In the kitchen, look for clues that they are eating. Glance in the fridge. Notice if there is food, and if it looks fresh.

Pay attention to this part: It is all relative. Look for that *change.* Do not overreact. One small change isn't enough by itself. It should just make you start looking deeper.

Some change is normal. However, if you see something that really concerns you, what do you do next?

Working together with your brothers and sisters, ask Mom or Dad if you might have a professional consultant like the VNA meet with all of you. Evaluations are free. They help determine what the issues are, as well as what needs are not being met. They suggest options and solutions. Maybe your folks just need some in-home help.

You can hire help with housekeeping and/or with personal care. A service can come in once a week to help with medication management. It's another set of eyes.

If you are strongly concerned, insist on scheduling an appointment with their doctor, and go with them.

Their safety is your primary concern.

So, when you go home, don't just fly in, run around for 3 days, then fly out. Take some time to stop, look, listen.

13   DON'T BURDEN PARENTS WITH CHILDHOOD HOME HANG-UPS

Have Mom and Dad started to drop hints that they want to sell the family home that they've been living in for 50 years – the home you grew up in?

How do you feel about that?

Last year I was at a big four-bedroom home, meeting with a husband and wife who were in their 80's. They said they had to move because it was just too much work to keep up, even though they had a cleaning lady and had hired someone to do all the yard work.

Walking through the house was like taking a trip back in time. The three kids still had their own bedrooms. Each of their rooms was reminiscent of the 1970's – right down to the stuffed animals and school trophies. These "kids" were now in their late 50's. Of course, when they would come to visit once or twice a year, they each stayed in their own room.

The couple told me that they had mentioned selling several times, but the kids had gotten quite upset. The son had actually yelled at her: "Mom, you can't sell our house!"

Are you burdening your parents? I say, it's time to grow up!

Sometimes we revert to our childhood roles when we go home. Take a good look at yourself. Are you weighing down your parents? Maybe your response is that you need somewhere to stay when you go home, so they might as well keep it the same. Really?

Sit down and have an open discussion with your folks. Assure them that when they are ready to sell "your" house, it is OK with you. Heck, you can even offer to start clearing your items out. Have you ever wondered if Mom might like to use one of those bedrooms for something else, but your stuff is holding her back? At this point, it is hard for her to ask you.

Do you know what I told that couple? I suggested they call the kids, be firm but gentle, and say it's time to sell the house. Explain that they need to move to an easier-to-manage home, and if any of the kids are interested in buying the house they can have first option.

In other words, buy it or be quiet.

Sadly, that son didn't speak to his parents for 6 months because they sold "his" house. He didn't even live in the same state.

There is a happy ending.

The mom called to tell me that her son finally came to visit them. She said that about an hour after he arrived and she had given him the grand tour of their new apartment, he suddenly gave her a gigantic hug. He apologized deeply and looking around her new home, laughed and said: "Mom, you gave us the best gift a parent could ever give their children – you cleaned out your own house!"

Kids, don't waste 6 months of your life. Talk to your folks. Even if they aren't about to start down that road, when they are ready, it'll be great to know that they have your blessing.

14   THERE'S MEANING BEHIND THE KAYAK

It had sounded like a simple move. "My parents are relocating to Arizona and we need an estimate," the woman had said over the phone.

Walking up to the ramshackle two-story house, I admired the wooded yard with a beautiful view overlooking the Fox River.

I was met at the door by Molly, a rather tense woman, with a barked greeting of: "Come in. Tell my dad he can't take his kayak to Phoenix!"

Inside, the house was in obvious upheaval. There were half-filled boxes and items strewn everywhere. It was easy to see that they were ripping the house apart for a quick move.

Stepping into the living room, there they all were — three adult children, all standing over Mom and Dad, who were sitting on the sofa. Mom was twisting a Kleenex in her lap and Dad was sitting there, red-eyed and tearful. The tension in the room was thick.

Molly aggressively repeated to me, "Tell Dad he can't take his kayak. They're going to Arizona. The kayak is not practical!"

I suggested we start with a walk through the house to evaluate what was moving and discuss their plans.

Molly took me through, pointing out what few items were moving. She explained that due to their health, the kids had decided that Mom and Dad were going to assisted-living in Phoenix. That way, they would have care, and Molly and the grandchildren lived nearby.

"Tell me about the kayak," I said.

"Well, things were going along fine until we got to that stupid kayak. Dad insists we move it."

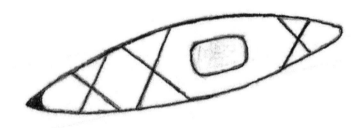

As we finished walking through the old house, we got back to the living room. Her dad looked up at me and pled his case, "I have kayaked the Fox River for 57 years. I'm not going without my kayak." Between the frustration and pain, he was actually choking when he said it.

Despite his words, I could tell he obviously hadn't been out on the river for several years.

I took Molly into the kitchen and we talked for a while about the many changes Dad was being forced to make just then. This wasn't really about a kayak. It was about having to say goodbye to things that meant so much throughout his life.

We discussed the possibility of them taking the kayak and storing at her house. Wouldn't it be just a minor inconvenience? The benefit was in preserving the value her dad placed on that memory.

Eventually, she walked back in the living room, went over to her dad, gave him a big hug, and announced: "Dad, we're taking the kayak!"

A smile lit up his face. After that, he willingly went along with everything else.

Do you know the "kayaks" in your parents' lives? When you are helping your parents make transitions, be respectful of the possessions they value. If possible, keep the items that have true meaning to them. If it isn't possible, still treat those items in a way that respects their importance to your folks.

They may be making a lot of changes in a very short time. Maybe not everything has to change.

15 TIME TO PUT YOUR HOUSE ON A DIET

Do you remember your first home? It started pretty lean, just a few furnishings. You got a bed from your parents, and added a sofa from a rummage sale.   You splurged on matching lamps to spice it up.

Perhaps Grandma gave you goodies - an old cherry kitchen set, some dishes.   You hungered for everything, because there was room to grow.

As you added to your family, you added to your house. With children came beds, dressers and bookcases.

Possibly you had a craving for elegance, and indulged in a dining room set – with a matching china cabinet.

Naturally, you added treats that you couldn't resist, like that entertainment center for the new family room in the basement. Maybe you even added a floor-standing TV that you had a hankering for.

When the kids were in high-school, your life was jammed with activities, and so was your house. The family room was bulging with air-hockey, furniture, games and stuff.

It still is. So is the garage. It's heaped with sports equipment and toys, not to mention Dad's toys. Yes, he has them all.

In the kitchen, Mom has every cooking utensil known to woman, even a bread maker.

Here you are now, in your middle years. The kids have moved out. Your house is bursting at the seams.

Is it time for your house to go on a diet?

Today, I'll share a recipe for your new, trimmer look.

From this day forward, it is about self-control, diet and exercise!

Self-control is about knowing when to stop. Reduce your intake. Nothing comes into the house, unless something goes out. Curb your appetite. Ask your spouse to go on this diet with you. There is power in doing it together.

Dieting is about weight loss. It is making appropriate choices about what you actually need in your life. Cut out those treats you've stashed away, the ones that add extra weight, but serve little purpose.

The exercise part of the program is *doing it*. Choose what you really use and love, and eliminate the rest. Ask the kids to haul out the old computer and lug excess furniture out of the basement.

Stretch yourself by using things for more than one purpose. Do you really enjoy and use the bread maker, or will a loaf pan do the same thing?

You have plenty of life to live. Don't spend it surrounded by items you don't use anymore. Shed those old clothes and clear out duplicate tools.

You may even choose to undergo radical weight loss. Consider the healthy changes that come with cutting out whole rooms, and moving to a smaller home.

Your leaner home will give you some unexpected benefits. Because you have less around, you will have more energy and extra time to do other things, to explore new hobbies. You will have less stress, and less work.

As we age, carrying all that extra weight becomes a burden. Get your house fit, and enjoy the new you.

16   MAKING FINAL WISHES KNOWN IS A GIFT YOU GIVE YOUR FAMILY

Moms, here is a Mother's Day gift you can give your family - and yourself. It's a simple envelope with a piece of paper in it. The title on the envelope is: My Final Wishes.

Ha! I suppose you're thinking, "That's morbid".

Not at all. Instead, think of it as a considerate way to do something now that will help your loved ones through what will be a very difficult and emotional time someday.

You will help them with a very tough future responsibility, and, possibly, you will save your family from arguing about what they each think is "how Mom would want it done." They aren't mind readers.

Several years ago, my husband was going in for a life-threatening surgery. At the hospital, they gave him a pre-planning list with things to do like make a will, a medical power of attorney and a living will... The last thing he wanted to do was fill out those forms, because it meant accepting that he might die. It's like bad luck.

Unhappily, he took the forms anyway.

"Hey, can we have two sets of forms?" I asked. "I want to make sure he knows my final wishes, too!"

Although we were married over 20 years at the time, we had never once talked about this taboo subject.

Since we tend to judge others based on our own perceptions, I was stunned when he stated matter-of-factly, "Of course, I want to be cremated."

"You better not cremate me," I said laughing at this difference from what I assumed. "I want to be buried at St. Mary's Cemetery."

That got us going on a lively and eye-opening discussion about what we each would like to have happen when we die.

My hubby's aunt gave us that gift, years ago. It was just such an envelope. What a blessing it was. She lived a hundred miles away, and when she unexpectedly passed away, there was a myriad of things to deal with, but her gift took us halfway there.

It was just a few details like her church, the funeral home she preferred, that she wanted cremation and a service and what to do with her ashes. We didn't have to guess, and believe me, we would have guessed wrong.

Moms, the "My Final Wishes" envelope is the first step. If you want to go a step further, make an appointment with your favorite funeral home. I went last week. Since I was writing this column, it seemed like the logical thing to do.

Do you know they'll sit down with you and help you plan what you want – and they don't charge for it? You can set everything up according to your wishes. Free. Yes, you can pre-pay if you want, but it isn't necessary.

I left there feeling good about my "future", because it's official now. It's documented. The best part was doing it when I had no trauma going on.

Looking back, if my husband and I hadn't talked that day, I'm pretty sure he would have cremated me, and I know I would have buried him at St. Mary's. Look how wrong we would have been about each other's wishes!

So, mothers, think about giving this gift. By the way, dads, Father's Day is just around the corner, too.

17 IT'S SPRING AND A GREAT TIME TO DO SOME HOUSECLEANING

Use it or Lose it! It's an expression that we've heard many times, usually in relation to our brain or our muscles.

Today, let's give it a whole new meaning.

Think about what is in your house — in your closets, in your basement and garage. Might there be something that you don't use? *Well, use it or lose it!*

I'll bet this isn't the first time you've thought about gathering some items for Goodwill or your favorite charity? Do you have a bag or a box around that you have started? Perhaps you started it last year. Or the year before. Have you filled it?   More likely, you started, then set it aside and have forgotten about it.

After you finish your paper this morning, let's get right at it.

Grab a garbage bag. Make a goal to put 20 things in that bag.

Start in the linen closet. Really, how many sheets and towels do you need? If the bottom ones have been there more than two years, you don't use them, so lose them.

Now, about your bedroom closet. I know how sensitive you can be about your clothes. Just take out six items that you don't use any more. Of course, if you get on a roll and want to clear some more, go grab another garbage bag, and keep going. Yes, Goodwill needs shoes.

If your sack is getting too heavy, grab a box from the basement. Surely you have a box you've been "saving" in case you need it. This is the time to use it.

Now to the kitchen cupboards. Do you have plenty of dishes for leftovers and storage?

Maybe you have enough storage containers and lids to make a stack 15 feet high. It's time to clean out.

Look in your pots and pans cupboard. Is there a pan you haven't used for 10 years? Help out a new family. Since you don't use it, lose it!

In the den, do you have books? My friend, Bud, works at Goodwill. He said they really need books. Share your love of reading with someone who can't afford to buy new books.

Ladies, let's go to the sewing room. Is there material that is faded because you never found the right use for it? You know what to do with it.

Gents, how about that work room? If you have a good set of screwdrivers that you really like and use, it's time to lose that set that you don't like. Setting up a toolbox can be expensive. Help out a new homeowner by donating your unused tools.

Oops, I forgot to mention one rule about our Use It or Lose It project — you shouldn't discard your spouse's items. Shucks, you have enough of your own clutter to work on. If you want them involved, give them their own bag and have a little contest.

Goodwill, or whatever your charity of choice, will appreciate your donations, and you'll feel better because you've started clearing out some clutter. It's freeing.

One more thing. When you are finished, it is imperative that you put those items in your car, and within 48 hours, take them to your charity.

If you don't deliver them, come Saturday, when you are ready to go to the grocery store, you'll take them back out of the trunk and put them in the garage for later. Later can quickly become next year, or the year after that.

OK, now, are you ready? Let's go!

18   SHARE THE CARE: AN ORGANIZED WAY TO LEND ASSISTANCE

I can't wait to share this with you.

Recently I learned about a program that can make your life easier, really.

So read on if you are taking care of a spouse, a parent, a neighbor or a friend, who is facing major health or aging issues that are so overwhelming for them that they need your help.

Read on if it is becoming so much for you, that you are finding your life completely absorbed by them and you wish you had someone to help. You may even find yourself crying for help. It's called "care-giver burnout" for a reason.

Read on if you know there are other family members/children/neighbors/friends who could help, but don't, or if their idea of helping isn't what you really need.

Read on if you can't think of anyone to turn to, but you know you need help.

You don't have to do this alone.

You can put together a group of people to help. It's called Share The Care. Today we'll see how it's done.

Ready?

First, do some homework. Don't read this and think you should just get some friends and family together to help. Nope. Learn about Share The Care, with their easy-to-follow, step by step model. Don't reinvent the wheel.

In the Fox Cities, Share The Care is taught by the Outagamie Caregiver Coalition. They provide education and support. Their flyer reads: "Share The Care is a way for friends and neighbors to organize a caregiving team to provide much-needed support."

The plan is also available on the official website at: www.sharethecare.org, or as I did, read the book: _Share The Care_, by Cappy Capossela and Sheila Warnock.

Basically, two key people learn about the system and coordinate a single gathering. That might be their only task. It should not be done by the person who is ill, nor by the primary caregiver. Ask someone else to do this. They will.

The Share The Care plan walks these two key people through the first meeting; who to invite, how to brainstorm on needs, how to find the best fit for each member - whether they live in town, or across the country; essentially, learn how to turn a diverse group into a functioning caregiving unit.

It is important to include the person receiving help. They need to know there are people who want to assist; they need to hear why people want to help them and why it is important to those people; and they need to articulate their boundaries, like "I don't want personal care, but I want you to visit."

We don't want to do this to them or for them – rather, with them.

Right now you probably have one or two people who are doing everything. There are so many tasks that could be done by others who want to lend a hand.

With forethought and organization, there will ultimately be an assorted group of caring individuals working together as a team to help the person with need. It will also free up the primary caregiver to concentrate his/her efforts where they are most needed.

To do List—
Wed - Rubbish out
Groceries
Pick up medicine
Doctor's Appointment
Pay bills

In the book, they say: "A little help can make a huge difference."

People want to help. Let them really make a difference.

19   HELPFUL NEIGHBORS MUCH APPRECIATED

What would we do without our neighbors?

Last week, at a family funeral, I was surprised to hear that one of our older aunts, who can't drive anymore, was brought from 50 miles away by her neighbor. Now that's going the extra distance.

Today, let's send a big shout-out to all the wonderful neighbors who make it possible for our parents and grandparents to live independently in their house longer.

Many seniors choose to stay in their family home, and as the workload becomes harder to do alone, it is surprising - or maybe not surprising - how their neighbors step up to help them.

We live in such a giving community.

Are you one of those neighbors? If so, thank you.

Just a few weeks ago, my out-of-town mother-in-law had us

a bit concerned when we called for several hours and got no answer. We phoned her neighbor, Ken, to check the house. She wasn't home, but he kept an eye out and when her friends dropped her off, he went over again and had her call us. She was just out having a great day with her pals. Thanks Ken.

Thank you to those neighbors who shovel the extra sidewalks, those who run the lawn mower around one more yard, and those who just hang out over the fence for a chat to help relieve those sometimes lonely days.

Thanks to Bill and Jan, who occasionally run Grandma to the doctor, and there is Lynn and Laurie who call when they are going to the grocery store to see if Ma needs anything.

Bless you neighbors who, just by your quiet presence, give us peace of mind knowing that our folks have a guardian angel watching out for them.

You see Mom or Dad in their daily lives, and often, are the first to notice when something just isn't right.

You let us know when you thought Grandma's driving was becoming questionable, because you noticed how she couldn't back out of the driveway anymore.

You checked when the light in Carol's den hadn't been turned off at 9 p.m. like it normally was. Thank God for you. She had fallen and the paramedics said she wouldn't have survived there much longer.

So today, my hat goes off to all of you.

I'd be remiss if I didn't mention, and you might be thinking it, that there are always goofballs out there who will take advantage of someone who is frail. Don't step over the line by ingratiating yourself so they might be generous to you. Don't convince yourself that you are helping them by taking items of value or that it gives them peace of mind knowing that their good silver is better off in your hands than their ungrateful family.

That being said, now back to my original thought - thank you, kindly neighbors!

Hopefully, I can live up to the example that you all have set.

20   LEAVING HOUSE FOR KIDS TO CLEAR OUT DOESN'T END WELL (PART 1 OF 3)

Parents often proudly tell me that they don't need to start clearing out their very full house. "The kids can take care of it when we are gone," they say, like it's a gift.

Well, it happened again. I heard another "dumpster" story.

Here's a typical example:

The parents lived in their home for 57 years. The dad died three years ago. The mom, "Dottie", fell a month ago and broke her ankle. She has been at a nursing home for rehab and will be released next week. She cannot go home alone.

The four children live in Appleton, Dallas, Minneapolis and Sarasota.

After a family powwow via e-mail and a conference call, they decide to move Dottie to an apartment for assisted living. The kids all fly into town on Thursday for a long weekend so they can take care of the Mom.

Over the weekend, they want to visit with Dottie as much as possible and include her in all the decisions so that the choices are hers.

A myriad of decisions are made in a short period of time. The kids select the community Dottie will move to, call in Realtors to list the house, hire us to move her and decide what to do with her car now that she can't drive.

Dottie is absolutely overwhelmed. Think of the stress on her - the commotion, the pleasure of having the kids visiting, the pain of watching her life dismantled, the pressure of making all those decisions, listening to the kids argue, and to top it off, she is feeling pretty rough because of her health.

Before they even come to town, the children agree that the house needs to be emptied out, and that this is the perfect time because they are all here. They order a dumpster for Friday morning.

They set Dottie in her favorite chair in the living room. They don't really have lots of time, so they just get at it. One son goes upstairs and works on the attic, the other son to the basement. The two daughters start selecting what will go with Dottie to the apartment.

They divvy up what each one wants from the house, which really wasn't much. They are in their 50's and 60's themselves and comment that they already have more in their own houses than they need.

As they go through, the situation gets a little frantic. There is so much work and so little time. When they pull something out to look at, they ask if anyone wants it. If not, they ask Mom what she wants done with it. More decisions.

There's lots of teasing. "Mom, why did you save this? It's junk!" Off to the dumpster it goes.

They throw out a life-time of her treasures. There are tears as Dottie is forced to go along with whatever the kids decide.

When the weekend is over, the kids are proud. They got everything accomplished.

What do you think? What choice did the parents actually leave the kids?

Next time, let's explore how this could be handled differently.

21   DON'T BULLDOZE MOM'S BELONGINGS FOR SAKE OF A SPEEDY TRANSITION   (PART 2 OF 3)

Let's look at an imaginary situation, and consider two different approaches.

At 85 years old, Dottie had been living alone in the family home since Phil, her husband, passed away. She recently broke her ankle and next week she'll be released from therapy. She can't go back home. It just isn't practical any more.

Her four kids are scattered around the country, and all of them want to come home the next weekend to help Dottie move to assisted living. The oldest, Brian, says they should also clear out the house to sell it, since Mom needs the money and they'd all be in town. Another brother offers to order a dumpster for Friday morning because: "None of the kids really want much", and, referring to the hooked rugs, said, "It's mostly junk anyway".

STOP!

This doesn't end well. Don't let expediency be an excuse to bulldoze Mom.

Instead, Ann, the local daughter, foresaw how stressful this could become for Dottie so she talked her siblings into a slightly different plan.

Ann hired a Senior Move Manager (SMM), who got a floor-plan for the new apartment. Then the SMM measured Dottie's furniture. With Ann, she helped Dottie decide what she loves, what will fit and what is useful. Together, they also chose her favorite decorations to make her new home cozy.

Movers took the selected furniture and treasures to Dottie's new apartment. The next day, Ann and the SMM decorated Dottie's apartment, taking special effort to make it feel like home.

When Dottie gets out of the nursing home, she will go directly to her new apartment and settle in. Once there, if she wants to change something, it can still be retrieved from the house.

When the family comes home for the weekend, Dottie can enjoy showing off her new home.

Together Dottie and the kids will spend the weekend looking around the old house and deciding what they would each like to keep - what a great opportunity for them to laugh, share memories and to say goodbye to their past.

It is arranged that on Wednesday, once the children and Dottie have removed what they want, buyers will come in to make an offer to purchase the balance of the items and clear out the house within a week.

The estate buyers are excited when they see the hooked rugs, and cringe when they hear the previous plans for a dumpster; they know that in their haste and ignorance, the kids would have thrown away items that would have meant extra money for their mom.

With a little sprucing-up, the house, one of Dottie's biggest assets, is ready to list.

Dottie feels comfortable in her new home, and she made the choices herself. Her treasures were handled with respect. Most importantly, she is now in a safe and secure environment where there is help to assist with her needs.

Next, we'll look at how Dottie and Phil, with a little planning, could have made this a smoother transition.

22   DOWNSIZING HOUSEHOLD BEGINS NOW   (PART 3 OF 3)

Last time, I shared a story about 85-year-old Dottie.   Her husband, Phil, passed away three years ago.   She fell recently and wasn't able to return to her house.   Instead, she was moving to an assisted living apartment.   The kids had ordered a dumpster and were ready to clear out her house.

When should someone start planning the transition out of the big family house?

Let's look back 35 years.

At 50 years old, Phil and Dottie are very comfortable in their home.   The four kids have moved out.   There is one grandchild, and another on the way.   One son has moved to Texas and visits occasionally.

Phil and Dottie say they are years away from starting to downsize.

At 60, Dottie and Phil are quite content. Phil has Parkinson's, but it isn't much of a problem. Three of the kids have moved out of state, but they usually come home over Christmas. One daughter, Ann, is in town and stops over often.

Phil and Dottie still have the four bedrooms set up because they get used occasionally, and they have the space, so why not?

Dottie enjoys having everyone together at the holidays. She beams with pride thinking of the memories she is creating for her family.

Dottie and Phil aren't ready to talk about downsizing.

At 70 years old, Phil's Parkinson's is getting progressively worse. Dottie has more responsibilities. She makes sure Phil gets his medications, runs them to doctor appointments, and she has more household tasks because Phil really can't help much anymore.

The family get-togethers are tough for Dottie. She still loves the house being the center of the family but finds the work to pull it off is exhausting. When the family comes, she pretends that everything is fine. Ann knows better and keeps talking to her parents about moving to an apartment so the workload on Mom will be much lighter.

Her siblings tell Ann to back off. Everything is just fine. They like having a place to stay when they come home, and to them it is practical to keep the house just the way it is.

At 85, the house is still full of everything - from the kids' old school papers to all the other things that were "too valuable" to get rid of.

So, when should you start clearing out your house and downsizing?

My answer is now, no matter what stage you are in. It is a life-process. You want to always be working on it, then it will never become overwhelming – or one spouse's problem.

Now is the time to start planning for the future. Now is the time to start passing the history of special items to the kids and grandkids. Now is the time to consider what you use and love, and start clearing out what is irrelevant in your life.

Talk to your spouse and your kids. Start a realistic plan, set goals, and get at it. You can control your future.

23 VETERANS PENSION AN OPTION FOR WARTIME VETS

Veterans Day is Friday, so I'd like to discuss a benefit for wartime vets that many are not aware of. It is the veterans pension.

For several years, I helped my buddy Phil with his finances. He lived on Social Security. They say you shouldn't plan to live off just Social Security but the reality is that many do.

Phil would get his check on the 5th. We'd pay the rent and utilities, pay something on his never-ending medical bills, and buy prescriptions, bus passes and groceries.

On that budget, buying the little things is tough; like a small Christmas gift for his grandchildren, an evening out with friends or new shoes.

Phil often teased about how he wished we could stretch it further so he could buy more of his Achilles' heel, Pepsi.

Sadly, a month after Phil died, I learned of the Veterans Pension. If you are eligible for it, I don't want you to miss the opportunity Phil did.

Roughly, here are some factors for determining if you are eligible:

1) Veteran's Pension is for veterans, spouses and surviving spouses of service members who served at least 1 day during a war period. They did not have to serve in the country of the war.

2) Veteran is over 65 or disabled (not from the service).

3) Must show financial need. Some of the main factors are: Low income, assets under $80,000 (they don't count your house) and medical expenses.
Yes, it starts out as simple as that.

Simple? Yes. Easy? No.

No one will come looking for you to give you this money. You must apply for it. Based on this brief information, don't decide if you qualify or not. Ask.

The paperwork can be tedious. But if you get $1,000-$2,000 a month, isn't it worth it? Even if the process takes a while, they pay retroactive to when you applied.

I spoke with Attorney Drew MacDonald, who you may know for his work with the Old Glory Honor Flight. He suggested you get an experienced advocate because at 70 to 90 years old, you may not be equipped to handle the paperwork at this juncture of your life. MacDonald is certified through the VA to help file for VA benefits. He said you should never pay a fee to an attorney, or anyone, to help you file.

Contact your County Veterans Service Office (CVSO). Their job is to help veterans and their families obtain veterans benefits, and they are happy to do so. It's not free money – you've earned it.

Looking back on the last years with Phil, and how he accepted the hardships that came his way, it would have been such a relief to have had more money; he may have even been able to keep the refrigerator stocked with Pepsi!

On this Veterans Day, make it a point to find out if you might be eligible and apply for the Veterans Pension. And to all of you veterans out there, THANK YOU.

Your County Veterans Service Office (CVSO) provides information and assistance in obtaining state and federal veterans benefits.

24   SHOPPING FOR ELDERLY PARENTS? WE'VE GOT IDEAS

What, oh what, do we get Mom and Dad, or Grandma and Grandpa, for Christmas?

They say they don't want or need anything, yet we still want to show we care.

I sent a shout-out to several seniors and caregivers. Here are their responses. Not one of them mentioned fancy coffee makers, nor LCD TVs, nor general "stuff".

A recurring suggestion was gift cards: Cards for gas, groceries, their hair salon/barber shop and for their pharmacy to help with co-pays.

One gent responded: "We still give my 95-year-young mother-in-law gift certificates to her favorite eating places. She loves to eat out, and even though we treat most of the time, she still likes to pull out a gift certificate and say, 'Let me buy dinner tonight.'"

One obviously techie senior suggested gift cards so he can get Nook books, or iTunes gift cards for his music downloads.

Another favorite is single-serving food, also soups, brownies, cookies and candy. One gal said: "My parents always loved home-cooked meals, frozen and ready to microwave, especially as it got harder for Dad to see to cook and for Mom to stand long enough to cook."

I laughed when one suggested finding them a boyfriend/girlfriend – "but only if they are alone", she quipped.

If they live in a community, check with the community about gift certificates for salons, additional meals and "banked" money for outside trips.

There is always a need for personal hygiene items and lotion. One friend told me: "When my grandma was in the nursing home, I would massage her hands with her favorite lotion. It kept her hands nice, it was a way to connect through touching and it was a scent she enjoyed."

More: Puzzles, stamps, box of birthday cards, and thank you notes, easy crossword puzzle books.

Give your parents the gift of independence with the push-the-button-for-help units. It can make them feel safe and allow them to remain in their house.

Help around the house was a huge response. Hire professional services or do it yourself. If you want to splurge, hire a service to shovel, cut grass or clean.

You could offer your assistance to: Clean closets, cook a meal, spring clean, shampoo carpets, clean windows, change furnace filters, or balance their checkbook and pay bills.

Not surprisingly, the number one request was giving the gift of you and your time.

Make a coupon book and say you will: Call them every Tuesday morning, take them to Friday night fish, do weekly shopping trips (grocery, clothes, window), take them to Sunday church service, have a movie night at their place complete with DVDs and popcorn, play cards/games, bring grandchildren to visit. The list could go on.

Keep in mind that it is more of a gift if you take them to *their* church service, play *their* favorite card game, or watch a movie *they* want to see.

If you give the coupon book, don't wait for them to take you up on it, schedule it. Commit to it. They'll have something to look forward to, and you'll share quality time with them.

Share this with your kids and encourage them to give Grandma and Grandpa something they can really use and enjoy. This Christmas, give a gift from the heart.

A couple more ideas from reader Sue: "Personalized calendars with birthdays and family events already noted.

These are especially nice for those with memory impairments.

Also consider medical equipment that could be helpful but they wouldn't otherwise buy for themselves, such as long-handled grabbers, hand-held shower attachments, microwavable heating pads, blood pressure monitors.

My parents are getting a BP monitor so that my Mom won't have to continue to go out in the winter to get it checked. I'm getting a pulse oximeter for my dad in the hopes that routinely checking his oxygen saturation levels can nip his recurring bouts of pneumonia in the bud before they get severe enough to require hospitalization. Not the most exciting gifts, but, hopefully, they'll be useful to them and help to maintain their health."

25   MOM IS A HOARDER WHO NEEDS HELP

Dear Jean,

Mom is a hoarder. It causes so much tension in our family. It's gotten to the point that all we do is argue about how awful her house is. She asks me to help her clean, but when I try, we just fight. Last weekend, I spent 3 hours there. I cleared lots out, but she dragged it back in. After all that work, nothing actually left, and now we aren't speaking to each other.

My brothers have just stopped going, and said they won't talk to her until she cleans it all. The grandchildren aren't allowed there because it is so nasty.

Now my brothers want to get her out of the house, go in there behind her back and purge. I'm torn. I think it is the only way to clean, but it seems mean.

Answer: Your instinct is correct. It is mean. Your mother will feel betrayed, and it won't solve anything.

It will cause her distress.

She will probably react by going out and getting more.

Real hoarding is an illness. If your mom had a broken leg, you wouldn't take away her crutches and insist that she walk.

She doesn't keep things because she is a poor housekeeper; nor because she doesn't care what it is doing to the family. This isn't about all of you kids. It is about her. Instead of trying to fix your mother's home, you need to help fix her heart. She is in pain.

Hoarding, often considered an obsessive-compulsive disorder, is a coping mechanism. It can be triggered by an emotional trauma, like the death of a loved one. The person can't control the emotional loss, so they become fixated on something they can control – the stuff; there is a disconnect in the thought process. They may even agree with you logically, but can't control the anxiety that it causes when they try to let go of things.

Stuff is safety. The emotions need to be dealt with. If you take all of her stuff away, you also take away her sense of safety and control.

Many of us collect clutter. It becomes a disorder when it interferes with life. You've stated some examples – not safe in her house, it causes conflict with the family, and she gets anxiety when you try to move things.

How can you help? The solution isn't cleaning the house; it is getting Mom emotional help.

Try to understand her. Encourage her to get counseling to explore why she collects things – ultimately pushing those who love her out of her life. The first step is that she has to accept that there is a problem and be willing to get help.

Keep planting seeds, take little steps. "Mom, we want to come over. We want to bring the grandchildren. We'll do whatever we can to help you."

For counseling, check with your family doctor for referral to a behavioral health provider, or contact the Aging and Disability Resource Center in your county.

Also, it isn't just her that needs counseling. The whole family needs help, because you are all suffering and need to understand how to help her.

Rather than a sneak attack, try to have her agree to just making the home safer. Ask her if you can clear walkways, stairs and fire hazards. Maybe she will offer less resistance when she doesn't feel threatened. Then stick to what you offered. Let her see she can trust you not to attack the fortress she has built.

Don't withhold your love and that of the grandchildren. Instead of going to her house, visit somewhere else, perhaps at a restaurant, at your house or at a park.

Your mom needs your love now more than ever.

26 VALUABLES OFTEN HIDDEN IN UNLIKELY PLACES

My English teacher at Wilson Jr. High, Mrs. Howard, used to talk about conditional sentences. You remember them: "If...., then...". If A is true, then B happens.

Folks, today let's have a little conversation about hiding things of value, and then consider the "If..., then..."

Recently I was chatting with other senior move managers about places we have found treasures in homes as we were helping pack and move our clients. Here are some places they mentioned:

❖   Money in a cookie tin under the living room couch.
❖   Diamond ring frozen into a pound of hamburger in the freezer.
❖   Money hidden in a hole in the mattress.
❖   Diamond ring in a pill bottle, put inside the leg of ironing board with the rubber foot put back on.
❖   Tin foil wads in freezer.
❖   One envelope was under the corner of the carpet.

- ❖ Packet of bills taped to the back of an old hanging shoe bag which I noticed as I was tossing the bag into the trash pile.
- ❖ In curtain rods, or sewn into curtain hems.
- ❖ Rolled up in an old sock at the bottom of a closet surrounded by bags of candies.
- ❖ 2-gallon plastic paint bucket in a pile of trash in the basement filled with 1,000 silver dollars.

- ❖ Books, magazines, clothes pockets, purses, car glove compartment.
- ❖ In the cat box under the liner, wrapped in plastic.
- ❖ In the bottom of the dirty clothes basket.
- ❖ Coins in a Ziploc bag inside the toilet tank.
- ❖ In the basement, a metal tool box was found filled with utility stocks worth $17,000.
- ❖ Under the drain pan of the refrigerator.
- ❖ "My stepmom hid her emeralds in the flour and sugar canisters and under the frozen peas. We tore the kitchen apart after she died unexpectedly, only to find she had recently moved them to her scrap yarn box."
- ❖ Stuffed into the toes of shoes and boots.
- ❖ Disco ball.

Disco ball, gotta love it!

I was smiling as I typed these. It really makes you wonder how many treasures are missed and gone forever.

If we agree that as we age, we start forgetting things (I know I do); and we want to make sure our assets are used to either make our life easier, or to pass along to our family – *then* it is in our best interest to tell someone where our hiding place is.

If you have trust issues, *then* put a note with your special papers that will be looked at when it is the right time. Do not put the note in your safe deposit box, which doesn't get opened right away.

If you hide things too well, *then* they will never be found.

Do I have that correct, Mrs. Howard?

27 MOVING COMES WITH PLENTY OF EMOTIONS

"Commotion and emotion." That's what a senior answered when I asked how things were going with downsizing and getting ready for her move.

Isn't that just it, in a nutshell?

At the end of this month, Washington Place Apartments in downtown Appleton is closing because the building no longer is livable. The 70 disabled and senior folks who live there are being moved to the new Riverwalk Place in the Eagle Flats Project.

As the Senior Move Manager® selected to handle the relocation of the residents, I've spent quite a bit of time there in the last two months.

Some of the residents are excited, some are frustrated, some are thrilled and some just go with the flow.

One fellow, Joe, spends a lot of time in the lobby watching the progress. His smile greets me every time I visit. Joe has lots of questions and always has a positive attitude.

Like many seniors who are making a transition, the Washington Place folks are going through commotion. And like many seniors, the changes are not coming because they chose them, but rather out of necessity. Take one move from a long-time home, and multiply it times 70 people.

Much of the commotion is because moving time is a very hectic time. The paperwork alone can be daunting. Look just at all the people you have to tell that you're moving. Then there is the cleaning, planning and sorting through years of treasures.

Fortunately, for the Washington Place group, the Appleton Housing Authority is helping with details like handling the movers, cable change-over and the documentation needed for various agencies.

The Kiwanis are helping some with the sorting of what does and doesn't go. Moving time is a great time to clean house, but if you aren't strong enough, it sure is nice to have help.

After the move in, a group of volunteers from several churches will help unpack and hang pictures. How nice that there are people in our community who will lend a hand when needed.

The residents are watching the progress of the construction at the new building. They know it will soon be home and wonder what it will be like. It will mean changes.

Typically, the more one can learn about what is happening, the less anxiety there is, so the residents are getting floor plans of their new apartment. With that they can think about furniture placement.

We have been meeting with them to answer all their questions, so they understand how the move will proceed. We want to keep them as much in-the-know as possible.

There is much emotion when saying goodbye to the something that is familiar, even when it isn't working well anymore, such as the elevators at Washington place, which are persnickety at best.

Our goal is to reduce commotion and emotion.

Like Joe, we should learn as much as we can to prepare ourselves for future changes. Ask lots of questions. Educate ourselves. And, like Joe, remember, it is just easier to approach the changes with a smile.

28 ALLOWING HELP CAN SAVE STRAIN ON YOUR CHILDREN

This week, two notes from my in box:

Dear Jean:

Do you ever deal with the extreme? Grandma has been fortunate to live on her own, and she is 90. Unfortunately, the family is overwhelmed helping her. We cut her grass, do her laundry, and take her to the doctor. We want to help her, but it is getting harder and harder.

It would be nice if she would let someone come to help with cooking and cleaning, but Grandma says she won't let a non-family member into her home.

Answer:

Hmmm.... Doesn't sound extreme. It sounds typical. Mom doesn't trust anyone to come in, so the kids have to do it all. What choice do they have? Either they do it or she suffers. The kids, who are being run ragged by their parents' very real needs, are begging for help.

There are an abundance of in-home services available, and they are such a wonderful help, but moms have to be willing to let them in.

Communication is everything. It's time to sit down and talk.

Hand your mom this column and tell her: "Mom, we love you and we want to help you stay in your home as long as you desire. We are doing as much for you as we can, but we are exhausted. We need your help."

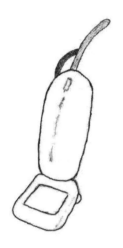

Then give ideas for areas in which you need help, like: "Let us hire some in-home services to lend a hand. We could start with two days a week, for a few hours, to help you clean, make a meal - they'll even take you shopping. Please."

Ask her to just "try" it for two months, which might help her fears subside. Also, agree if it doesn't work, you can try something else. That will give her some control and choice.

Then, the first couple of times, be there when the companion comes over.

Moms, they are asking for your help. Don't automatically say that you can't afford it. Can you afford not to? The children need some respite, and, I promise you'll start looking forward to your new helper's visits.

Dear Jean:

When my wife and I moved, we thought we had gotten rid of many things, but low and behold, we found out differently. People wait too long to get rid of 'stuff' because neither the husband nor wife wants to give up their valuable belongings. If they only knew that one valuable lesson in life is: 'You cannot take stuff along when you leave this place called earth.' It has really no value when all is said and done, only memories.

We have been at an apartment with assisted living for a year, and considering my condition, we should have done it three years ago, because I really couldn't help my wife and children with the move.

We knew few people when we moved, but have gotten to meet a lot of wonderful people. Also, there are many activities, so we can be involved in them if we choose.

Tell people that making new friends increases life spans, because finding people that you have something in common with adds vitality to your life."

Answer:

I don't need to tell people. You said it well yourself.

29   TALK ABOUT END OF LIFE

Dear Jean:

I cannot get my children to help me put together my final wishes. I told my daughter the only gift I wanted for Christmas was to sit down, talk and write out some health care instructions. Instead, she gave me a legal form in my Christmas card, and said she didn't have time right then. That was over a year ago. My son won't even talk to me about it. He said it's creepy. I just want to have a conversation about my wishes. What can I do?

Answer:

Call your daughter, read her this column and tell her it's time. Schedule an appointment together; if you include your son, all the better.

It isn't unusual for your children to avoid the subject. You might even hear, "We don't have to talk about that right now." It's like, "If we don't discuss it, you'll never die."

Of course, they are wrong. There is no better time to talk about it than when it isn't an urgent matter.

April 16 is National Health Care Decision Day. Why that date? Just a hint, there are two sure things in life: taxes and death.

Once your taxes are finished, it is time to start thinking about the second one.

Make it your goal to get it done this month. Tell the kids that when you have completed a plan, you'll have peace of mind.

It can be hard, but it is important.

I chatted with Sandra Potts, director of Fox Valley End of Life Care Coalition. One of their goals is to get families talking about end-of-life choices. She has some ideas for you.

The first step is to think about the last stage of your life and how you would like it to be. Here is a helpful website: www.TheConversationProject.org On the site, there is a conversation starter kit, which is non-threatening and walks you through the process.

Second, talk to your family, so when the time comes, they will know they are doing the right thing because they will have heard it from you.

If you do nothing else, you should talk to your family.

Third, decide who you would like to make decisions on your behalf if you can't. This is your health care power of attorney.

If you all talk together now about your wishes, when the time comes, your HCPOA should, hopefully, have the full support of the rest of the family because everyone will know what you want. It removes the second-guessing, the guilt and anxiety.

Discuss and fill out the form together. You don't need to spend money or get an attorney.

I applaud that you want to do this for your family.

They can't respect your wishes if they don't know what they are. At a time of trauma, they won't have to make choices for you. They will know your wishes and will be carrying out your choices.

Having this conversation isn't creepy, it's practical.

You said you want your daughter to do this as a gift for you. Someday your family will realize they are the ones who received the gift.

30   DON'T LET DIVVYING UP POSSESSIONS BREAK UP THE FAMILY

More questions from my inbox:

Dear Jean: My siblings live out of town, so it's left to me to keep an eye on Mother and take her to doctor appointments and the grocery store. How do I ask my family to chip in for gas money without getting them mad?

Answer: When you are worried about how they will interpret your request, do it directly, not by e-mail. Use "I" statements, rather than "you". An example might be: "I'm happy to take Mom to her appointments and errands like the grocery store. I could use help to offset the cost of gas. If you would help me with $20-$30 a month, it would really be appreciated. "

You don't just want one check sent to you. Note that there is a suggested amount, a range, and a time frame.

Maybe they're looking for ways to help.

Dear Jean: I'm furious with my brother. When we cleared out Mom and Dad's house, we took turns picking things because it seemed the most fair way to do it.

My brother picked the silverware that belonged to my Grandma. Then he sold it. How dare he! It should have stayed in the family.

Answer: Slow down. Take a breath.

Some family members are more sentimental than others.

Yes, it would have been nice if the silverware had stayed in the family, but if that was the expectation, it should have been made clear ahead of time.

In all fairness, the items you picked were yours to do with as you please. You could keep them, sell them or pass items along to your children. He gets the same privilege.

He may have picked something based on resale value. He gets to. It was his turn.

Further, I'll bet you weren't surprised by what he did. Was it consistent with his personality? Did you think: "How typical of him. He only cares about money, not history"?

If so, offering to purchase from him anything that he might sell could have avoided this. And yes, if he told you a fair price for the silverware, then that is what you should have paid him. You want to keep an asset; he wants to sell an asset.

This should not be interpreted as: If child A wants a sofa; and child B doesn't want anything; then B is entitled to cash. No.

Helping actually clear out the house helps the estate. I enjoy families that take turns picking and say "no passing on your turn".

Let's move on to the real issue here. Breaking up your parents' house can be a very emotion-filled time. Don't let it break up your family.

Enjoy your selections, and in your heart, forgive your brother for his choices.

My mom has a sign in her kitchen that reads: "The best things in life aren't things at all."

Fight against hurt feelings and mend your friendship with him. Make your parents proud that you were able to get through this difficult time with your family intact. Your relationship with your brother is far more important than things.

31   FOR SENIORS, SELLING HOUSE IS PERSONAL

"Is this the right time to sell our house?", I was asked by an 80-something couple.

I smiled because my next appointment was with a Realtor. "I'll ask her," I replied.

Sara Schnell, of Coldwell Banker, was quite enthused about the difference of selling a senior's house.

"With seniors, the question really shouldn't be if this is a good market to sell their house." She explained, "Selling your house isn't really about the market right now; instead, look at where your health is at, at your spouse's health and how much effort you want to keep putting into maintaining your home. Then ask, 'Is this the right time for us to sell our house?'"

"Houses are still selling. It's a matter of price. Are you going to make money? It depends on how long you've owned it," Schnell said. "Do we want to make the most money for you?

Absolutely. But you need to also factor in the time it takes to sell."

Schnell talked about today's buyers. "Your kids' generation isn't your market; they already have a house and are down-sizing themselves. Your market is your grandchildren's generation - that is who is buying three- to four-bedroom houses, and their world is very different."

Once seniors have decided to sell, how should they prepare their house?

"First," she emphasized, "Declutter. Pack what you want in your future home, and then give your kids any treasures they might like. If you can't afford to do anything else, cleaning out the clutter is by far the cheapest."

"Next, make the house less personal. Remove your family pictures. It isn't about decorating for what you like, it's about what will sell the house."

I asked about carpet, paint and wallpaper, mentioning that the seniors I just left had 3 bedrooms with worn, shag carpet. They want to give a carpet allowance. Is that a good idea?

"No. Younger buyers want to move right in, with little fuss. It is better to put neutral carpeting in if you can. You will get a faster sale and more money. Removing wallpaper and painting are also relatively inexpensive."

"You have so much competition. Buyers are looking at 15 to

20 houses. If yours is the one that involves work for them and it isn't their taste, they'll choose another house."

"This is your home, but you've already made a decision to move on. If you are financially able, decide where you want to go and move there. Get on with your life. To sit in this house while it is being marketed is so stressful for you and your spouse."

"But, shouldn't the seniors leave their furniture for staging?" I asked.

Schnell's answer: "No. It is too generation specific. In these strange economic times - vacant homes are more appealing. With the young buyers, even if they see their parents' furniture (50-somethings), they think it is dated. If they go into a house that is empty, they can better imagine themselves there."

When you decide the time is right for you to sell, price it right, market it right and get on with your life.

32 GETTING PAST THOSE PACK-RAT TENDENCIES

Here is another note from my in box:

Dear Jean: Thanks for the words of encouragement in letting us know we're not alone. I've always suspected that part of my Mom's pack-rat tendencies come from growing up extremely poor during the Depression, when nothing ever went to waste. Do you see that in other people as well?

Answer: Big time! Our parents were brought up constantly being told that they shouldn't throw anything away. Can't you still remember your grandpa saying: "Save that, you never know when you might need it."?

He said it because things were scarce back then. If they got a package in the mail, the bonus was the cardboard box it came in. And if the box was wrapped in string, all the better. They saved that box and string because they would find a use for it.

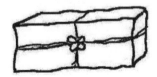

Of course, back in the 1930's and 1940's, they might have only gotten one box delivered in a year.

Times changed, but habits didn't. They are still saving those boxes and strings (and lots of other things). Deep down, they even feel proud when they stockpile something, because they know their dad is smiling down with approval, that they remember what he taught them.

Now, saving all that stuff leads to clutter. More comes into the house than goes out.

Our generation, on the other hand, thinks everything is disposable. Most of it is. Nothing lasts, and even if it does, things are often quickly outmoded.

Look at our music. In just 25 years, we have gone from record players to 8-track tapes to cassettes to CDs to iPods. I don't even use my iPod anymore. It's all on my smart phone.

You might pick on your parents, but I'll bet you have an outdated computer or TV sitting in the basement right now. I know, I know, you're going to get around to it.

That is just my point.

Keep in mind where our parents are coming from. Picking on them for holding onto their treasures is mean.

Parents, if you've been saving a toaster box for so long, that you no longer have the toaster, let it go. If you bought new pillows, but moved the old ones to the back of the closet, let them go.

Adult kids, you could actually offer to help.

For your elder parents, one of the hardest parts of clearing out the extra items in their house is doing the physical labor. The hard part for the kids is that they can't make the decisions for their parents on what should go.

Here is a project you can all do together. Kids, give your parents some blue painters tape. Suggest that at their leisure, they should go around the house and put it on anything they would like to have disappear, then offer to come back on a specific day and remove everything that is stickered. No judgments, no arguments – just help.

The kids and grandkids can haul out all marked items, whether to take items home themselves, or to pass things on to someone else or to put them in the garage and schedule a charity pick up.

Then, show up on the day you promised. Mom doesn't want tape on her furniture for 2 months. That isn't help.

Mom and Dad will really appreciate it.

33   REMEMBER, 'OLD' DOES NOT MEAN 'WORTHLESS'

For 50 years, Dad's letter opener sat on his desk. The metal handle is the shape of a lion, and there is about a 6 inch blade. It is solid.

When we were little, Mom and Dad ran the delivery business out of the house, so their desk was literally the company headquarters. That letter opener has always been next to our phone and the day book.

Mom would sit at the desk to answer the phone, and schedule customers. It was where Dad would open the mail, and, I'm sure, sometimes pray there was a check in there.

Even as children, we knew how to answer the phone properly, and take a message from Sid at the Fair Stores, Don at Montgomery Wards, or Pete Heid at Heid Music, all whom Dad delivered for.

We also knew how important the schedule was. We never played with the day book or fiddled with the tools on the desk. We always treated the desk and items on it with respect.

If the pen wasn't there when needed, how would Mom have taken the orders? We didn't mess with the letter opener either. We might have used it as a staple remover or a screw-driver, but then we put it right back.

Well, it's 50 years later. The company office is in an actual warehouse.

That letter opener rests on my desk. Yes, the handle is dented and the metal is rubbed smooth in some spots. The blade, well, that is pretty banged up too. I use it every single day. It is solid. I love that letter opener.

Recently, a sales rep was at my office trying to sell me something. As we were talking, he picked up the letter opener and said, "Why do you have this junky old thing? Can't you throw it away?"

Nice.

It really got me thinking.

As we age, we all want to continue to feel useful. Like that letter opener, we've got bumps, dents and some rough edges, but we still have a purpose. We still want to be treated with respect.

These days, it seems we equate "old" with "trash".

Are we really saying that things that are aged and worn should automatically be replaced? How many times have you asked Mom why she has some old item in her house, even referring to her possessions as junk?

Possibly those items hold strong memories for her, and she is willing to overlook their flaws, because their history means so much to her.

You hurt her feelings, and she wonders if you feel that way about her, too. But she just holds it in.

Think about what message you are sending. Be careful that you don't make your parents feel worthless. They aren't ready to be thrown out. We all want to feel wanted, needed and useful.

As for that sales rep, he sure annoyed me. He will just have to peddle his goods somewhere else.

34   IT'S EASIER TO DOWNSIZE NOW BEFORE YOU HAVE TO LATER

This was a tough week.   Not so much for me, the one watching, but for my customer, Joyce.

Joyce is 89.   Her husband passed away last year, and she is moving to Ohio, to be near her daughter.

Of course she'd rather stay - here in the house they raised their children, here where all her friends and family used to be, here in the world that she lived in 20 years ago.

That isn't an option.   Life has changed. When she moves closer to her children, they can help her, and she'll be able to see the grandchildren more often.

Joyce called me in because her house is so full that she is overwhelmed.   She can't do it alone.

Clearing out her house is agony for her.   It's a big, painful job.   In tears, she told me: "We should have done this long ago, so it wouldn't be so hard. We never got rid of anything because we had the space. It was so easy to just let things go on."

Sound familiar?

Well, a couple weeks ago, I was on WHBY's Good Neighbor radio show, with Kathy Keene.

A 50-something gal called in asking how to downsize. She said she's been married 32 years and has a full house. She was thinking about downsizing, and asked if it's better to start in the basement, or the attic?

Hmmm. I struggled trying to express that we don't help with downsizing. Afterword, I wondered why I had a problem with the question, since that is literally what we do.

Meeting with Joyce this week really put it in perspective for me.

I realized Boomers use the word downsize to describe clearing out things that are excess. They have usually reached a point in their life when they have too much stuff and know that they should do something about it.

So on one hand, we have Keene's caller. In her 50's, she has choices. If she downsizes, she would be getting rid of things she doesn't use anymore. It will still be manageable for her, if she chooses to do it now.

Joyce, on the other hand, waited. Now she is in the midst of something totally different, let's call it critical downsizing. That is where life takes a turn. Due to health changes or the death of a spouse, the person must leave the house they have been in for eons. The workload is overwhelming. It can be a gut-wrenching time. Choices become limited.

So readers, choose today.

Make a conscious effort to clear things that aren't part of your now. If it isn't a part of your life anymore, it is time for it to go. Now, while it is easier.

Change your shopping habits. Tell yourself, from this day forward, if you bring something into your house, something goes out. And mean it.

Today you can control what happens to your future. Get going. Do a wonderful thing for the 'you' that is yet to come. You will thank yourself for it.

35 SPEAK UP IF YOU SUSPECT ELDER ABUSE

If you think your elderly friend or relative is being taken advantage of by someone, and you do nothing, you are causing them harm.

Let's look at an increasing way our seniors are being taken advantage of.

The elements are all there. Start with the decline in the economy, add rising unemployment, and then add that seniors often have significant assets. The result is an increase in adult children moving in with their elderly parents.

In most instances, it is a real win-win. The adult child helps Dad with meals, caregiving, keeping the house clean and respecting his wishes. In return, the adult child has a roof over their head, and the comfort of knowing Dad has the best care they can give him. That is when it works well, as it so often does.

What sounds like a dream solution can sometimes become a nightmare.

If the children that move in to the parents' house don't respect them, it can lead to trouble.

They may justify taking Dad's assets with reasons such as: "It will be my money someday anyway," or "I deserve a trip to Vegas because of all the things I do for him," or even "He should buy me a motorcycle because the government will get his money if I don't spend it."

Diane Mandler, a supervisor at Outagamie County Adult Protective Services, shared with me some of the signs of exploitation:

o You are kept away, or supervised when visiting. By isolating Mom, she can't tell anyone what is going on.
o She appears neglected; her hygiene is not kept up.
o She is being over-drugged, or has food withheld.
o Large sums of money are disappearing.
o There are changes in the household that Mom probably isn't comfortable with.
o Mom's peace is disturbed. Things just aren't normal.

Perhaps, if you quiz your relative or friend, they may deny that anything is wrong. They may feel alone, especially if they have been repeatedly told that if their care-giver doesn't look after them, no one will. Fear is a way to control someone.

If you think an older person is being exploited, contact Adult Protective Services. One call can change everything.

You are not sticking your nose in where it doesn't belong. We take care of each other. Right?

APS will make an unannounced visit to the house and do a welfare check. By law, your identity is kept confidential.

If issues are found, APS can help reduce the danger. They offer options and solutions of how to combat the problems. Your friend will get help if they accept it. Even if they don't, their abuser is on notice that they are being watched.

If the situation isn't resolved immediately, don't be discouraged. Because of confidentiality, APS can't discuss with you what is going on. Keep at it. Sometimes they need to build a case. Keep them notified of problems.

We are a community. We take care of each other. If you suspect that someone's care-givers aren't working in their best interest, let a professional check it out.

Be the voice of those who are vulnerable. Everyone has the right to live with dignity.

36   SHARING FAMILY MEMORIES IS JUST A SNIPPET AWAY

Christmas is just around the corner. Let me share a special gift you can give to your parents, your children, your grandchildren, and your brothers and sisters. And it is free. The only cost is literally a minute or two.

To give you some background, the biggest challenge my senior friends have when they start downsizing, is that it is hard to let go of things. To them, they aren't just stuff. All those items are full of memories; with those memories come deep emotions.

I'll use my dad as an example.

Dad always had a special beer stein that he kept on his shelf. Even as kids, we knew it meant a lot to him because we weren't allowed to touch it. Ever. I always thought Dad had picked it up at some souvenir shop in Germany when he was part of the occupying forces after World War II.

For him, it doesn't just hold beer, it holds memories.

It got me thinking. Wouldn't it be cool if there were a way to make a video of Dad telling the story of that stein, a quick little clip, maybe 50-60 seconds? You know, just a snippet.

It would be a way to preserve the memory for him. Even if the stein was ever broken, he would still be able to see the snippet. If he ever passed it on, the next person would know the history.

Naturally, my next thought was that I would want to share that snippet with my brothers and sisters. They would remember it from our parents' house and enjoy Dad telling the story.

Suddenly, it dawned on me. Folks, we have a way to make those snippets. It is right at our fingertips. It's our cellphone. And you're already guessing the next part - we can share with your family by Facebook or YouTube.

I asked Dad to let me shoot a video memory of him telling about that stein. We did it, just 51 seconds. He enjoyed sharing, and I enjoyed hearing. Then we got on a roll. We filmed 47 seconds of him talking about a family picture, and then another 63 seconds about how he and Mom met. Mom joined the fun and we shot 54 seconds of her story about her grandma's platter.

My next step was to create a YouTube link to share with my sisters. (Be sure to use the privacy setting "unlisted", so only people with the link can view it.)

Well, the joke was on me. In just those 51 seconds, I learned things that I never knew about that stein. Let's not ruin the surprise; you can see for yourselves.   Would you like to meet my Dad? Here he is: http://youtu.be/R44bPWhFmEM

Now you have your homework assignment.   This month, when you are together for the holidays, do it.

When will there be a better time?

Make, share, enjoy.   Make 20 of them.   Make a family "scrapbook" of snippets. Get the kids and the grandkids involved. You can add to your collection for years to come.

Make it a very Merry Christmas!

37   ADULT CHILDREN NEED TO SET BOUNDRIES, SEEK OUTSIDE HELP

Dear Jean:

You often give advice about downsizing and moving into a community. I totally agree, but my parents are so stubborn. They won't even discuss it.

They said they are staying in their house. At 60, I am so tired of the workload. I have a full-time job waitressing and my own house to keep up, yet I'm running to their house all the time: cleaning, doing laundry, getting groceries and taking them to doctor appointments.

My husband is 62 and is retired. Even though he has started having issues with his heart, he cuts their grass and does their yard work. Winter is coming, and I don't want my husband shoveling anymore.

I want my parents to go to a senior apartment. How can I make them move?

Answer:

You can't.

You made me smile, though. Similar to how we can give our adult children advice but they do what they want, your parents get to decide where and how they live. You might not agree with them. That's OK.

You can prod, encourage, educate and present options; but the choices are theirs. They have free will.

Note to readers: If your parents are not capable of making rational decisions, then that is a whole different discussion.

Look at what elements of the senior apartment living you most want them to have, and help incorporate them into their house.

Is it about safety? Things can be done to make their house safer. Possibly you or a professional can install grab-bars. Get emergency help buttons and have the clutter on the stairs cleared off.

Is your concern about having extra help with everyday tasks? There are many in-home health care agencies available. They do chores like laundry, vacuuming, running errands and can even take your parents grocery shopping. As an extra benefit, they are great for companionship.

You can't control your parents' choices, but you can choose how you will deal with their requests.

You can set boundaries. Put a limit to the amount of work you and your husband do there. Helping your parents stay in their home is wonderful, but shouldn't wear you out.

This isn't a measure of your love.

Have a heart-to-heart talk with them. Discuss what services they can pay for themselves, and what things you will do. Perhaps they can hire a yard service. Share that you would be happy to take them to medical appointments because it is helpful to have a family member along, but that they need to find help with household chores.

Often, they will talk about the expense. If they can afford it, but don't want to spend the money, be firm. If they don't have the money, try to discuss ways to reduce the load.

Just because they want the grass cut every week, does not mean you are the one who has to do it. They have made the choice to stay there. What would happen if the grass wasn't cut?

In their generation, our parents were raised to save, save, save. Remind them that they've saved all their life so they could have a comfortable retirement, and now it is time to use that investment on themselves (and on your health).

38   ASHES TO ASHES: FINAL RESTING PLACE DESERVES RESPECT

Here is my best shot at delicately covering today's topic, hopefully with a light touch.

Last year, as a moving consultant, I was walking through the house with a 40-something gal, Laura.   Because it was a corporate relocation, my job was to coordinate the transfer of her household goods from Wisconsin to Dallas.

When we were in the furnace room in the basement, there were shelves with camping gear, Christmas decorations and odds-and-ends storage.   Laura pointed to a box on the floor: "That's Uncle Jim."   She said with a smile, "He wanted to be buried where his sister is, down in Chicago.   We're supposed to get the family together to do it, but everyone is always so busy."

Then she further explained, with humor, "We keep him by the furnace, because he liked to be warm."

I was a bit taken aback. It somehow felt disrespectful to keep a person's ashes on the floor in the basement.

"Oh, my goodness," I smiled in response, "You're moving away to Texas in a month. When do you think there will be a better time to take care of him?"

Then I suggested: "Why not call the cemetery and make arrangements to mail his ashes? You could have him buried as he requested, then the family can always have a graveside gathering sometime in the future."

Later, I told this story to Janel, one of the women who helps me clean out houses. She wasn't surprised and shared that when she was cleaning out an estate, she found two urns of ashes. Janel called the daughter and asked where to send them.

The daughter responded: "Those are some relatives. I don't know who. Can you just throw them in the trash?"

To which Janel responded with a firm "No, I won't."

Of course, not everyone shares my view, so I asked a funeral director friend, then called a cemetery, and even my church.

They all had very definite ideas of what should be done with cremains, and all of them used the word "respect".

This isn't about just a box of ashes, rather it is about the final resting place of a person, yes, a human being.

When you bring cremains into your home, it is a temporary solution. Even if you keep them in a special place on a shelf, it is still temporary. Eternity is a long time. Eventually, there needs to be a final resting place.

Whatever, wherever that place is, it needs to outlive you, so others aren't left dealing with it for you.

If you have ashes in your house, waiting to get around to placement somewhere, resolve to get it done.

If you are planning to be cremated, be sure your family knows what you want done with your ashes.

A couple of months after Laura moved to Texas, she called me and said thanks for nudging her. Although they haven't gotten the family together yet, Uncle Jim is now with his sister.

Laura said she has a huge sense of relief that it is done.

39 IT'S TIME FOR WORDS WITH GRANDMA

Sometimes the unknown can cause anxiety.

When you are a senior and living alone, if you don't know when you will hear from your family, it can be stressful. You sit and wait for them. And wait, and wait.

Last summer, when 30 year old Sam stopped in to see his grandma, she told him how much she missed her (adult) grandchildren, and that she never hears from them.

She got really choked up, telling him how they are all so busy, and don't have time for her.

Now mind you, not one of the grandchildren lives in the same city she does. All are over an hour away. Some are three to four hours away. They really do visit when they can.

She misses her babies. They may be all grown-up, raising families of their own, and busy with their careers, but she's lonesome.

Sam thought back to the previous week and remembered the many posts he had seen on Facebook from his cousins and his sister. They shared pictures of their kids, their trips, and all the goings-on in their hectic lives.

He came up with an idea, and when he got home, he sent them all a message.

"We do not make enough time for Grandma. She loves us, and needs to hear from us more."

"If you have time for '*WORDS with friends*', you have time for words with Grandma. I know you all have smart-phones." He told them, "Everyone pick a different day of the week, and then put it in your smart-calendar to call her, that way the calls are spread out. I'll take Wednesdays."

Surprisingly, they all quickly responded and chose a day. They've been calling her ever since. And Grandma loves it.

Instead of wondering, she hears from them.

Not only does this work for Sam's grandma, but here's another time it can work well.

Do you know someone in a nursing home?

Have you ever gone to visit Grandpa and someone else is already there? It's probably Sunday. He got two visitors in one day, but it might be another week, or two, until he gets another.

Without knowing when others are visiting, you might assume someone else is stopping in more often than you are, so your absence isn't a big deal.

With all the social media available, you can solve this dilemma, and make sure Grandpa is well taken care of.

How about creating an on-line calendar just for Grandpa, so everyone can see the available (lonely) spots?

How about the groups you belong to? Whether you are in a Rotary Club or a bridge club, you can easily organize visits for one of your friends who is in long-term care. Pass a paper calendar around the room and let everyone who is interested, pick a day. Your friend's month will quickly fill up with visits, instead of the big gaps between smiling faces.

Working together to make a schedule means Grandma will never have to question again whether her babies miss her as much as she misses them.

40   IF NOT YOU, THEN WHO?

Mom will tell you I was a bit of a collector in high school.

The walls of my room were covered things that had special memories. There were game programs from eighth grade basketball at St. Mary's, the pom-poms from my stint on Wilson Jr. High drill team, my 2nd place medal from the ice skating races at Jones Park.

The walls were plastered with souvenir everything — corsages, posters, Appleton West High School report cards and concert programs from the Cavern. I even kept my racing skates hanging on the wall.

You get the idea. Nothing was too silly to hold onto.

Mom came in one day and demanded: "Jean, if not you, who is going to clean this room? If not now, when are you going to clean it?" Then she informed me that I had the weekend to clean up my room — or, (the big threat here) or she was going to do it herself.

Surely, she wouldn't treat my very unique mementos with the special reverence they deserved. To her, it was all just "stuff". I knew I had to get it done.

Isn't that where we are all at now, 40, 50 or 60 years later? We've just spread out where we have our keepsakes. Now it's a whole houseful.

We have mementos from every decade: Items from our youth, from our children, our past hobbies, things from parents, from trips; we have a lifetime of collected stuff. Our house is full of memories, as well as scads of stuff we have no real use for.

Ask yourself: If not you, who? If not now, when?

If not you, who should be responsible for clearing out your house, and what happens with your personal items? If not now, when in your life will you be more able to do it?

How can you do it, you ask? It's so much. It is overwhelming.

Well, start!

Like my room in high school, it doesn't really help if you just take everything down off the shelves, dust them, and put them back up. You must actually make an impact on the volume.

Share items with your children and grandchildren. Pull items out, relive the memories, and then get things gone.

The local nonprofit thrift stores like Goodwill and St. Vincent de Paul are begging for items to put on their shelves.

I'm sensing a win-win here.

Indeed, I do know how hard it is to clean out special things – I still have my racing skates. They are part of me, even though my brain knows I'll probably never put them on again. Notice, I said "probably".

I am still in denial.

It is OK to hold dearly to very special items. But maybe it is time to hold on to less of them.

Like when listening to Mom's warning, clean your rooms now, while you can. Be responsible. Take care of the distribution of your special items and mementoes. You know no one will handle them with the same respect that you will.

41   COMPASSION CAN BE PRACTICED AT ANY AGE

Boy Scouts learned it early.

It wasn't just about walking that little, old lady across the street. That was actually the third step in the process of being compassionate.

First, before that Boy Scout put his arm out to guide her, he had to be *aware* enough to even see there was a little, old lady at the corner.

The second thing he had to do was to realize she was having a difficult time trying to cross. He had to feel what she was feeling – to *empathize.*

Only then, was he ready for step three – *doing* something.

You don't have to be a Boy Scout to be aware of what's going on with your folks, to empathize with them, and to do something to help them.

Are you aware of the challenges facing your parents? Before you answer "yes", really think about it.

I don't mean from your prospective, I mean from theirs. Is there something weighing down on them? Can you lighten their load?

Then help them.

No, it doesn't mean you have to do it yourself.

It means you should help make it happen. Think creatively. You don't have to cut their grass, but you can help them find someone who will do it on a steady basis.

No, it doesn't mean you have to agree. You can disagree, kindly.

We helped a gentleman move to a retirement community. The next morning, he was anxious because he didn't know where he was when he woke up. He wanted to go back home. His son agreed and immediately moved him back. The son surely felt he was being compassionate.

There is more than one way to show compassion. I would suggest that the son could have chosen a different route. He could have been aware that his father was stressed, could have empathized with his dad, and then could have done something different, like reassuring his dad that he had made the right choice to move to a safer environment. He could have encouraged his dad to give the new home a try for a month or two.

Yes, simply listening and encouraging is also being compassionate.

Don't go directly to step three and start doing things for your parents. If that little, old lady didn't need, or want, to cross the street, then the Boy Scout might not have been helping her.

Also, be patient. This isn't a one-shot deal, when you solve one issue, you then move on to the next opportunity.

The Appleton Compassion Project exhibit just finished. Perhaps you heard that we had over 10,000 grade school students who decorated tiles that showed what compassion meant to them. The project was based on the belief that compassion can be learned as a skill.

We can be part of the Compassion Project, too. We can continue to be a role model for our children and/or grandchildren. We can do it by showing them how we treat our own parents with compassion.

42 DEALING WITH DEMENTIA REQUIRES A CHANGE IN THINKING

Dementia. Alzheimer's. Those are some scary words.

Recently I attended a great program, and would like to share just a few key ideas with you. It was called Coping with Challenging Behaviors in Dementia Care, presented by Jason Schmitz, RN, owner of Heartwood Homes Senior Living, and an expert on dementia care.

Schmitz's first point was that in the early stages of dementia/Alzheimer's, loss of control can be a big concern to your parent. Don't take normal tasks away; keep them involved whenever possible. If there are past-due bills that aren't getting paid, don't take over the job, instead, work with Dad. Maybe, let him write the checks. You can help by stuffing and mailing the envelopes. Let him still retain some control.

Second, as the disease progresses, Mom/Dad's reality changes. Their past becomes their present. They are actually living in their past. It is their current reality. They've changed how they think, so you need to change how you think.

Quit explaining the same thing to your parent over and over again. It causes them unnecessary stress. If you find yourself saying "Mom, don't you remember, I already told you ....?" Stop!

Enter their world, their reality. Learn to speak their language.

This is a new culture for us. We are so accustomed to parenting and correcting errors. Do you tell Dad he is doing something the wrong way? Not in his reality. Instead of correcting the behavior, ask yourself if there is a reason he is doing that, if it is from the reality he is currently in. Change your own approach to make this a win-win situation.

When you visit, develop a so-what attitude. If what they are doing isn't a risk to them or others, so what? If Dad keeps picking up papers and stacking them, so what? Maybe he was an accountant, and it's normal. Taking away the papers without distracting him or replacing the task with something else can cause frustration for him.

Don't forget to bring your sense of humor to your visits.

Another of Schmitz's lessons was that when you do go to visit, remember routine is security. Taking someone out of his or her schedule can be stressful. If you fly into town and have a big day planned of shopping, lunch and casino, you can really upset Mom's routine, which can cause her anxiety.

You can still have good times. Instead, spend quality time doing activities she enjoys and are at her current ability and interest level. Keep things calm and comfortable. Smile.

Consider simply validating what they are feeling. Try it a couple times. If Dad asks you where his sister Judy is, what need is he trying to fill? Either fulfill the memory or distract. If you respond with, "Dad, you know she is dead. Remember?" It doesn't accomplish anything. Instead, try validating his feeling, like "I understand that you miss her. Tell me about Aunt Judy." Ask questions about her. Instead of correcting, move on.

Remember, they are trying the best they can. You're the one with the healthy brain.

Further in the progression, you may feel it isn't worth visiting your parent. Two out of three times Mom may get your name wrong. So what? You're still fulfilling her need to have her hand held that day, the human need to be hugged, to talk with someone. Just being there to soothe her is a gift.

She still needs human contact in her life. Who better to give it to her than you? She still will pick up on the voices of her children, their touch.

She doesn't need you less, she needs you different.

43   CLEANING OUT WHAT YOU DON'T NEED IS THE NEXT PHASE

What exactly is "home"?

Throughout our lives, whatever place we live in, we sort of build our nest. We surround ourselves with things we use and love. Whether it's a dorm, an apartment or a house, we make it our home.

We start with the *Hand-Me-Down* phase. When we move into our first place, we'll gladly take just about anything from anyone. We barely care how it looks or how rickety it is because we need everything. Grandma's old couch is a treat, even if it doesn't match our rug.

We're happy to get Aunt Mary's four old kitchen chairs, although one has a broken seat. We'll fix it someday.

Then we move into our home's *Growth* phase. We upgrade our things to better match our needs and our style. As our family grows, so does the amount of stuff in our house.

I remember when we comfortably had the money to buy a full set of matching dishes to replace all the cast-offs we had in the beginning. I felt like a homemaker goddess!

In the *Growth* phase, we still take hand-me-downs, but only if they are better than what we have, and we want them to match our taste. We might buy a new sofa. We move Grandma's now even older couch to the basement.

Aunt Mary's chairs go into the storage room because they really are cute, and someday we want to refinish them.

Next is the *Established* phase. Our home is filled with items that really are us, that reflect our personality. We have things that we need and that we love. We've also collected just about everything we might potentially have a use for, and lots that we don't.

Well Boomers, what's next? The kids have moved out, and our lifestyle has changed. We don't need all that space, nor all that work — and we still have all that stuff. Aunt Mary's chairs are still in the storage room.

Most of us are heading into the *"What's Next"* phase. Your parents might be there too. Do you criticize your parents because they have too much stuff in their house?

Don't judge them, understand them. They were at the stage you are in now, but then more time went by. They didn't tackle downsizing when they had the energy, and now it is overwhelming.

So, are you going to decide *What's Next* for you, and start working toward it? If it is your house, be ruthless! If it is your parents' house, be kind and helpful.

Talk to your own kids. If they are past the *Hand-Me-Down* phase, don't be annoyed if they don't want Aunt Mary's chairs. You never got around to fixing them, so what makes you think they will? They didn't even know Aunt Mary.

When downsizing, think about the difference between the things that are just stuff and the things that you really use and love.

Keep building your nest, but sometimes we build anew by clearing out what we no longer need.

Only you can decide *What's Next* for you.

44 WORK ON A UNIFIED PLAN TO AID AGING PARENT

This past month has been tough for a family I'm working with. Here is their story:

The mom is having some major health issues, and for several reasons, she can't stay in her duplex anymore. She agrees that it is time for her to move, yet she wishes she could stay. The change is hard.

Her daughter, Sandy, lives two hours away, and has been prodding Mom to move somewhere so she will be secure and has help when needed. Besides Mom's health issues, the neighborhood has been changing, and Sandy is worried about her mom's safety.

When Mom finally agreed to move to assisted living, Sandy was relieved. She has made several trips in the past month to help her mom select what moves and helped distribute the rest of the items to family.

From Sandy's perspective, she knows that although she is missing work a lot this month, soon Mom will be all set, and there won't be as many worries. She is Mom's rock.

When I stopped in on Monday, Sandy was fighting back tears as she privately told me that her older brother, Chuck, called from California and talked to Mom over the weekend. Sandy said that in one fell swoop, Chuck sabotaged all her hard work. He had told Mom that it wasn't right that Sandy was making her move, and she should stay in the duplex.

Can you see Chuck's perspective? He hasn't been home for more than a year and hasn't seen all the health and environmental reasons for this move. He just knows his mom is hurting and he wants to support her.

The emotions are really getting to Mom, and Sandy and Chuck.

The difference here is that each person is approaching this change from a different point of view.

At a seminar I recently attended, a similar situation was discussed by Karen Dorn, co-owner and mediator at Alternative Resolutions.

Dorn talked of how family dynamics are like a puzzle. "Everybody has their own pieces, but none has the big picture, and the only way to get the whole picture is to bring it all together."

In this family's situation, none of the parties are totally wrong. None of them want to be difficult; they just each have different pieces of the puzzle.

Rather than giving Mom two messages and pulling her apart – what if the kids and Mom had first started by putting all their ideas together and had a unified plan.

Perhaps they might have set a goal: "We want Mom to be safe and well." If the three agreed on how to achieve the final result, they would all be working toward achieving it.

As Dorn explained, "Now that the whole picture is together, decisions can be based on complete information rather than just a portion."

When you are helping make decisions with your parents, remember that each member of the family has their pieces to contribute, and working together, you can make this a smoother transition.

45   DEPRESSION IS NOT A NORMAL
PART OF AGING

When you look in the mirror in the morning, what do you see?

If you are over 60, you may see a person in pain. Are you losing interest in activities you used to enjoy? Do you feel hopeless, helpless and empty? Possibly you've had a change in appetite, declining energy and trouble sleeping.

Older adults often have changes in their life that don't necessarily cause depression, but can certainly trigger it.

National Depression Screening Day is in October, so I chatted with Kristine Sack, older adult counselor from Lutheran Social Services.

Sack explained: "Some things that are particular to seniors are major life changes such as loss of a spouse, moving from the family home, sense of being a burden and even loss of a pet. As one starts to rely on others to do things they used to do themselves, such as driving or needing a walker, it can be a real knock to one's self-esteem."

"These situations naturally cause depression," Sack said. "With grief and loss, of course you will feel sad and lonely for a while, but if it persists and you can't shake it, and it becomes long term, you might start thinking it is normal. It isn't."

Consider getting help to get you through it.

If this sounds like someone you know, talk to them honestly and openly. Ask the question: "I know you've had some losses, that you are having trouble keeping weight on, and you tell me you don't sleep well at night. Do you think maybe you're depressed?"

The response you might get is they aren't depressed, just feeling down. People have a picture in their head about what depression looks like, but when they look in that mirror, that's not what they see.

Talking it over can be good therapy, but an untrained friend might try to be helpful with "just snap out of it". That's like telling someone having an asthma attack to "just snap out of it". It can't be done. Don't you think they would if they could?

There are two things that can help. Medically, many family doctors can prescribe anti-depressants and people respond very well. Outcomes are better if you are evaluated by your doctor, and you add talk-therapy. You can do one or the other, but if you do both, you will have better results.

"Part of it is a generational thing. We don't want to air our dirty laundry," Sack said. "This isn't a moral issue, it's a medical issue."

"Depression is not a normal part of aging, and it shouldn't have to be accepted. People sometimes suffer in silence unnecessarily."

If you think you or your loved one is depressed, get some help. Ask your primary care doctor for an evaluation, talk to your religious advisor or therapist.

"Two-thirds of people who are depressed don't seek necessary treatment, although more than 80% of all cases can effectively be treated with medication, therapy, or both."

Nothing can improve without taking the first step. By allowing some extra help, when you look in the mirror in the morning, you'll see a person who is feeling stronger, hopeful, and more engaged in the world around you.

Need help?   Contact your local
Aging and Disability Resource Center

46 DON'T CLING TO STUFF YOU NO LONGER NEED

How do you catch a monkey?

Long ago, an interesting way was to let them catch themselves.

Hunters would make a hole in a coconut, put pieces of oranges inside and then hang the coconut from a tree.

As the monkey came around, it would catch the sweet smell of the oranges and reach into the hole. Once it grasped the orange, it wouldn't be able to pull its hand out of the coconut. It caught itself. It could be free anytime, but it wouldn't let go to save its life.

How like a monkey we can be sometimes. Do you find yourself holding on to "stuff" that actually impedes your life?

Marilyn Ellis, billed as America's Organizer Coach, put together a humorous, yet true, list of reasons we give ourselves for holding onto things:

- I paid a lot for it.
- It's not good enough to keep, but it is too good to throw out.
- I might need it someday.
- My kids might need it someday.
- My grandkids might need it someday.
- It's inherited, it's ugly, but I don't want to be the one to finally get rid of it.
- It might be worth something.
- It holds a lot of memories.

Earlier in our lives, we were trying to fill spaces in our homes. But once we have filled all those spaces, many folks just keep bringing things home for all those reasons listed, and more. Gasp! When do you stop?

As we move into smaller places, it is time to reprogram our thinking.

When one is seriously down-sizing, the list of reasons for holding onto things is much shorter:
- Does it bring me great pleasure?
- Is it practical?

And yes, because it reminds us of a cherished memory can be a reason to keep something, but perhaps not 36 of that something.

Yes, paper toweling is practical, but 21 rolls of it? Take two.

Look at each item you are considering, and have a spot in mind for it, like, "this will go on the kitchen counter."

The greatest mistake I see my customers make when they down-size, is holding onto too many things that are irrelevant.

No matter what size place you are moving to, think about where the items you are taking will be put.

Start out your new home with instantly comfortable and enjoyable surroundings by hand-selecting items from your old house that are practical and give you pleasure.

Don't be a monkey, holding onto those oranges that keep you from living a comfortable life. Let go of those things that hold you back.

47   IN-HOME CARE FOR A PARENT IS A CRUCIAL DECISION

It's Christmas. As a gift, are you considering setting up in-home help for your parent?

What is it? Should kids help set it up? Should parents accept it?

"It's like the four wheels on the car," describes Denis Ashauer, owner of Home Helpers. "In order to function well at home, people must be mobile, eating well, able to take medication, and able to make good decisions. If one of those is missing, you're going to end up in the ditch."

In-home help keeps folks on track. That help may be running errands, doing laundry, grocery shopping, making sure meals are eaten and, importantly, being a trained set of eyes watching for parents' safety.

Something else, that isn't valued enough, is companionship.

"Well, it costs too much," I've heard people say.

"Really?" Ashauer said. "Compared to what? If it increases your ability to stay in your own home longer, isn't it is worth it?"

"One barrier," he pointed out, "is that this generation did everything themselves. They changed their own oil, cut their own lawn. They didn't pay anyone to do things."

"On the bright side, people who have paid for it, are a lot more accepting of services, because they've invested in it. Long term care insurance covers it."

VA benefits may cover it, too, depending on the individual case.

I told Ashauer that I sometimes get letters implying adult children are selfish, saying, "*I was willing to sacrifice for my mother, she raised me.*"

"Well, good for them," he replied, "But we're all living longer. It used to be that parents would live to 60 or 70 years old; now it's the 60- to 70-year olds who are taking care of their parents. Now the kids are the ones getting hip replacements. They're getting tired."

Maybe it is time to get it out in the open. Mom, we need your help. We love and care for you, but you need to help us, too.

Folks say they don't want strangers in their house. Ashauer's response: "After several visits, the relationship becomes stronger and they really start looking forward to it."

Conversely, seniors can go from not trusting, to too trusting.

If you hire an acquaintance, because they are cheaper than professional services, some things to consider: Have you run a criminal check? How is their driver's license? Is their car insurance paid? They are being put in a trusted position. What if they ingratiate themselves? Do they have any training, so they know what to look for if health is declining?

When someone is an employee, they bring all those things that cost the business money – worker's comp, taxes and liability insurance.

So, is hiring in-home care a good Christmas present?

The real question is, what is best for all of you? Perhaps sitting down together and talking with your parents is the gift.

You can't decide what your parents need; they have to decide what is right for them. And parents, a gift to your children is to consider doing your part to help them out.

48   TELL THEM YOU CARE

The words we never say.

You know them.

Say them. Now. While there's time. They can't hear the words if you don't say them. Allow no room for doubt or for regrets.

Pick up a phone, pick up a pen or get to the keyboard. Say it.

Mom, I love you.

I love you for making me the person I am today. I love you for taking me to school the first day and for not taking me to school the second day. I love you for teaching me good penmanship – by making me write 100 times "I will not pester my sister", soon followed by "I will not talk back, swear…"

I love you for teaching me how to keep house and be responsible – by making me vacuum, do dishes, cut the grass, do the laundry, cook. I hated doing chores instead of being outside. Thank you.

I love you for teaching me how to care for others, starting with my sisters and brothers, even when I didn't want to play with them, or let them tag along when I was with my friends.

I love you for teaching me how to say please and thank you, how to treat others with respect.

I love you for taking me fishing and camping. For the hikes through the woods and the fields. You showed me about beauty in a flower, in a butterfly, in the moon and stars.

The world is a beautiful place because you taught me to see it. Enjoying a glorious sunset reminds me of you.

Dad, I love you.

I love you for making me the person I am today. I love you for letting me play with your hammer and nails, even when it wasn't cool to let girls work with tools. I love you for taking me to your Jaycee outings and showing me that when you give to others, you receive something special, too.

I love that you punished me; firmly but fairly. OK, maybe I didn't love it then, but you taught me to be a good parent: firm but fair.

I love you for teaching me the value of money. I saw how hard you had to work to support the family, and know that "money doesn't grow on trees".

Daughter, I love you.

I love the reflection of me I see in you. I love your independence, your ability to take care of yourself, and how you care for those around you. You are a strong woman and you make me proud.

I see you with my grandchild, and know she can't go wrong with your love and guidance.

Son, I love you.

I love the man you have become. I love your strength, and your gentleness. I even love your weird sense of humor.

Seeing how you treat your wife and children, I know the future will be good. Watching you care for your grandparents, I feel blessed by your kindness. You are a good man and you make me proud.

If your loved one is already gone, know with conviction that they loved you. Have no doubt. Remember the warmth of that love, even when it wasn't spoken. Don't regret that it wasn't said enough. Go forward remembering the love they showed through their actions.

Now is the time. Tell them you love them. They need to hear it. You need to say it.

49   DOCUMENT ITEMS IN CASE OF THEFT

Dear Jean:

We recently had to deal with the possible theft of my mother's jewelry. Between the in-home caregivers, visitors and family, we didn't know who might have taken it. Before we made any accusations, we searched long and hard.

After much worry, fortunately we discovered that nothing was missing. It was merely misplaced by Mom who has memory issues and keeps moving things.

Some families aren't so lucky. Please offer suggestions on how to handle suspected theft, and also how to catalog valuables, especially items of worth such as art, jewelry and stamp/coin collections.

We don't know what we should have done if the jewelry really had been gone.

Answer:

I'm pleased to know that all ended well. It is great that you did a thorough search before accusing anyone. As you found out, if you had blamed someone, you could have been very wrong.

If a person suspects theft, the first step, which you did, is to hunt through the house, question Mom and quiz the family. Then contact your police department and your insurance company. Remember though, just because you suspect something, doesn't make it so. Nor does it automatically mean you can collect insurance on it.

As explained to me by an insurance adviser, Curt Fritz from Ademino & Associates, unless you have a rider added to your insurance policy, theft is usually limited to a low amount, like $2,500. That is not per item, but for the full loss. To purchase a rider, you need an appraisal, which is where a professional person documents the value.

If your mom has jewelry of very high value, and doesn't use it all the time, encourage her to keep it in a safe deposit box.

Let's look at how to document the valuables.

Fritz recommended a quick and easy way to catalog your mom's home.

"It doesn't have to be complicated," he said. "Record a video of the house and possessions. It's an invaluable tool to help you remember what you have.

"In just 15 minutes, you can record all the rooms, walk over to items of special value and hold them up to view on the recorder, even turn them over to show their markings. You can talk and provide more detail."

For the police, if things are stolen, having a photo and any significant markings or inscriptions are always helpful in locating the items down the line if pawned or recovered.

If you do the video on your smart phone, record a snippet of each room, then stop and record the next one. Later, you can easily send them to anyone.

It is good to have documentation of what is really in the house. Memories fade, and Mom may not remember that she gave something away months, or years, before.

It helps keep down family squabbles. You've got a record and all can easily review it.

Be sure to keep a copy somewhere other than the house.

Because it's quicker to do than writing a long list, you could do it this week.

50   MEMORIES OFTEN WILL DETERMINE 'REAL' VALUE

The grandpa was sitting in the living room. He reminded me of a cat, napping in the chair, enjoying the afternoon sun.

Lately, his world had become a bit fuzzy.

In the kitchen, we womenfolk sat around the table, drinking coffee and making plans. I was meeting with three generations of their family: Grandma Viola; her 60-something daughter, Amy; and 30ish granddaughter, Heather.

We were discussing the challenges faced now that Grandpa's memory was declining.

Viola was all business. "I hate to leave my house, but it doesn't work anymore," she said. "There are too many steps here and I'm afraid of him falling."

They had a two-story house with a basement. There were four steps outside, down to the driveway.

She had decided to move them to a senior apartment that offers assistance.

We had already gone over the first part of what I help folks with, the floor plan. We had discussed what items would be practical to take, and what would turn the apartment into their new home.

Another part of my job is to help families with how to then distribute/clear out what is left behind, whether it is to give items to children, to sell, or to donate.

This is a difficult topic because what seems like stuff to one person can be filled with memories for another.

I mentioned to Viola that sometimes the silliest things hold the most meaning for us, and that there's no way for her to know what items hold precious memoires for her family. I suggested that she simply ask them.

As an example, I turned to her daughter Amy, and asked, "What item in this room means the most to you?"

Looking around, Amy smiled, pointing to the apple-shaped clock on the wall. "I love that clock," she said wistfully. "It's been there forever. It reminds me of Mom because she was always in the kitchen when I came home from school, and she was always baking something wonderful."

Viola tut-tutted, "Amy, you don't want that old thing." Then proudly she said, "I am saving my crystal candle-sticks for you. I paid a lot for them."

I actually could see Amy groan inwardly. She smiled and graciously thanked her mother.

Then I asked Heather what she saw in the kitchen that was special to her. "The Cookie Monster cookie jar!" She replied merrily. "Grandma always has yummy cookies for us."

It was clear that Grandma didn't like the idea of her legacy being a cookie jar.

We moved to other topics and continued planning for the move.

An hour later, as we were at the door, and saying our goodbyes, Viola suddenly said: "Wait!" then excitedly, "Amy, please take the clock. I want you to have it. And Heather, let's go get that cookie jar right now, there are even some cookies in it."

All three burst out in big smiles and hugged each other. Arm-in-arm, they headed back to the kitchen.

I left, and I was smiling too.

ABOUT THE AUTHOR

Jean Long Manteufel has lived most of her life in her hometown of Appleton, WI. She graduated from University of Wisconsin in Green Bay in 1989 with a B.A. degree in Business Administration. Her major in Human Resources and minor in Sociology reflect that she enjoys working with people.

Manteufel is involved in the community as a business owner. Her hobby and joy is volunteering.

She is part of a close-knit family, most of whom still live within ten miles of the old farmstead. Manteufel enjoys spending time with her husband, children, grandchildren, brothers, sisters, parents, in-laws, aunts, uncles and cousins galore.

For more info, or to order more books, go to:
www.TransitionsWithJean.com